GRAPHIC FORENSIC SCIENCE

SOLVING CRIMES WITH
TRACE EVIDENCE

by Gary Jeffrey

illustrated by Peter Richardson

rosen publishing's
rosen central

New York

Published in 2008 by The Rosen Publishing Group, Inc.
29 East 21st Street, New York, NY 10010

First edition, 2008

Designed and produced by
David West Books

Editor: Gail Bushnell

Photo credits:
4&5, Andrei Tchernov; 6t, New York City Municipal Archives, 6m&b, National Library of Medicine; 7t, David Waugh, 7m, National Library of Medicine; 44, sx70; 45, Chris Hutchison.

Library of Congress Cataloging-in-Publication Data

Jeffrey, Gary.
  Solving crimes with trace evidence / Gary Jeffrey ; illustrated by
Peter Richardson. -- 1st ed.
      p. cm. -- (Graphic forensic science)
  Includes index.
  ISBN 978-1-4042-1431-6 (library binding) -- ISBN 978-1-4042-1432-3
(pbk.) -- ISBN 978-1-4042-1433-0 (6 pack)
  1. Criminal investigation--Juvenile literature. 2. Forensic
sciences--Juvenile literature. 3. Fingerprints--Juvenile literature.
I. Title.
  HV8073.8.J44 2008
  363.25'62--dc22
                                    2007044040

This book is produced using paper that is made from wood grown in managed, sustainable forests. It is natural renewable and recyclable. The logging and manufacturing processes conform to the environmental regulations of the country of origin.

Manufactured in China

CONTENTS

FINDING EVIDENCE

The evidence gathered at a crime scene can take many forms. Sometimes it is so small it is barely visible. Often, as in the case of fingerprints, it is invisible until revealed by a process.

INVISIBLE PROOFS

Crime scene investigators (CSI) have well-developed methods to help them find traces of blood, fingerprints, fibers, and other foreign material that may be present at a crime scene.

These physical clues are collected and sent to forensic science laboratories for further study. (Forensics is an examination of material, that is detailed enough to be presented in a court of law.) The forensic workers will also compare their fingerprint files, trace fibers, and blood sample results with previously gathered examples held in national databases.

Often trace evidence will form a vital part of a police file, undermining a suspect's alibi or proving they had physical contact with a victim when they had denied it. In these cases, trace evidence is often referred to as a "silent witness" —convicting criminals through what they left behind.

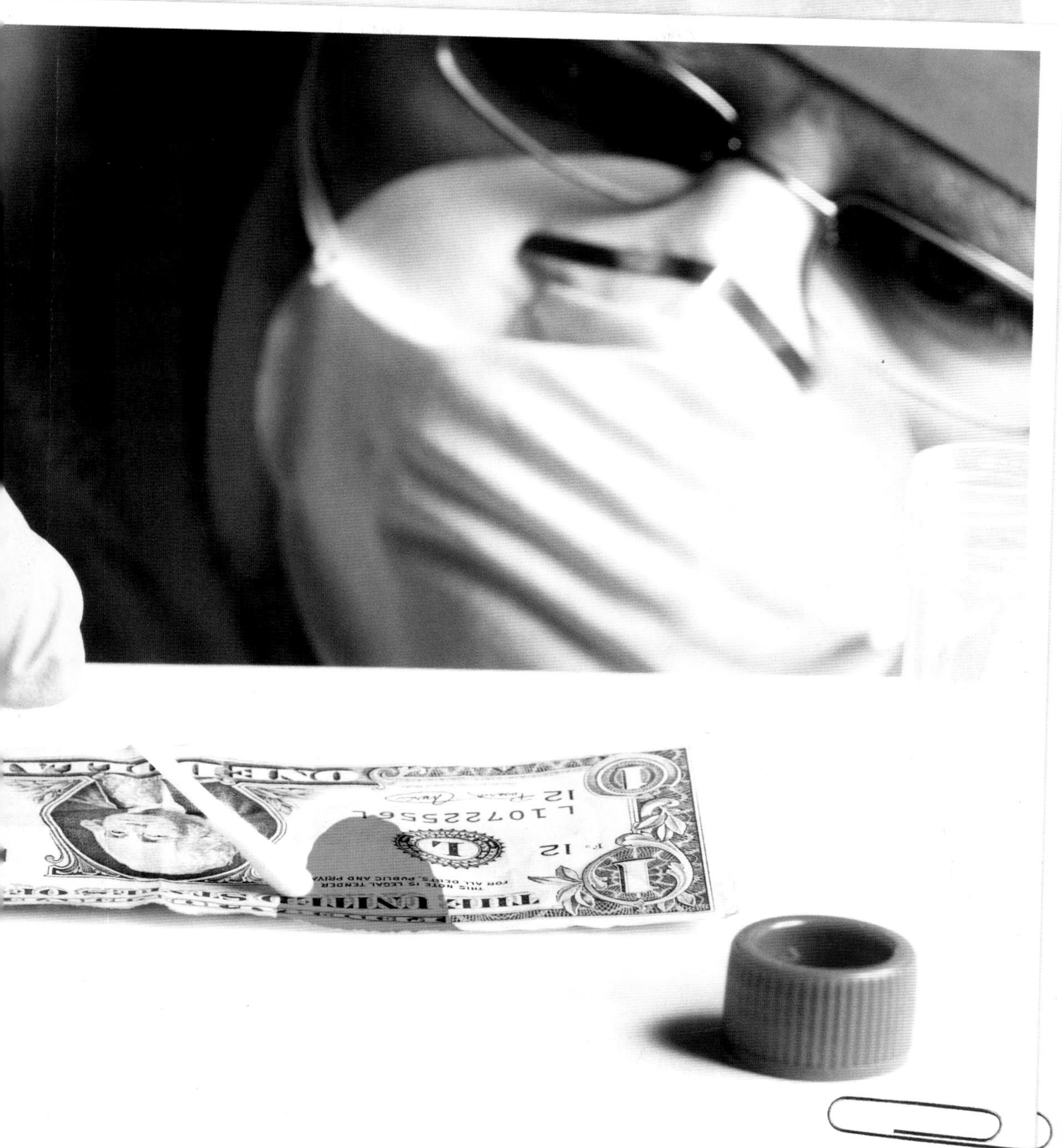

Blood is just one kind of trace evidence. CSIs have special chemicals that can reveal where blood has been even when it has been washed off. Blood itself will contain valuable information about who left it, through its DNA profile.

THE SILENT WITNESS

Early in the 20th century a scientist, Dr. Edmond Locard, put forward a theory—that every contact a person makes with another person or object leaves a trace. "Locard's Principle" is the basis for much of forensic science today.

A turn-of-the-century Bertillon card. The subjects' measurements were written on the back.

FINGERPRINTS

Locard's teacher, Alphonse Bertillon, invented the first criminal identification system in 1880. Based on the measurement of eleven bodily features, it was complicated to record. The police were attracted to the idea of using fingerprints alone, but didn't have a way of classifying them.

The problem was solved by an Englishman, Sir Edward Henry, in 1900, and by 1910 "The Henry System" was being used by police forces worldwide.

The computer age has further revolutionized fingerprint detection, enabling the enhancement of partial prints and fast searching and matching through vast databases.

From 1892, the right thumbprint of Francisca Rojas, the first criminal to be identified by fingerprints.

The method of taking fingerprints has changed very little. The tools used are printer's ink, a roller, plate, and paper.

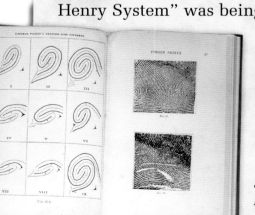

"The Henry system" divides fingerprints into groups based on pattern types. The three main patterns are called arches, whorls, and loops.

Under the Microscope

Microscopy was first used in a murder case as early as 1847, when minute pieces of a woman's scalp were found on a pistol butt. Human hair varies greatly around the body. Carpet and other fibers show distinctive characteristics when magnified. Unlike eyewitnesses, this physical evidence cannot lie or forget.

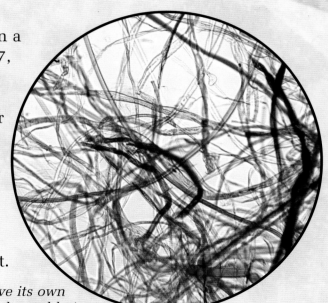

Each household's dust will have its own telltale mix of fibers, minerals, and hairs.

Plate V.
A B C D E F
1
2
3
4
5
6
7
OXY-HÆMOGLOBIN.
REDUCED HÆMOGLOBIN.
ACID HÆMATIN
BLOOD AFTER EXPOSURE.
BLOOD AFTER LONGER EXPOSURE.
REDUCED HÆMATIN.
AMMONIATED CARMINE.
ABSORPTION SPECTRA.

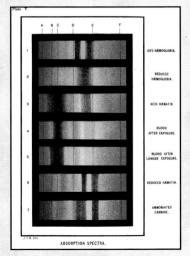

The analysis of light given off by burning different blood samples is called spectroscopy.

Blood and Other Bodily Fluids

The study of blood evidence is called serology. In the late 1900s, blood could be tested for the presence of toxins using a spectroscope. A test could also show the presence of bood, and in 1901 blood types were discovered. However, a breakthrough came with the discovery of DNA in 1953.

DNA, a person's individual genetic "blueprint," is present in every bodily cell. In 1987, the first criminal was identified and convicted using his DNA profile as evidence. The latest techniques can use material gathered from a single cell.

BRL
K562
BRL
4437-M
4437-C
4437-AF1
4437-C/AF1
BRL
4455-M
4455-C
4455-AF1
4455-C/AF1
BRL

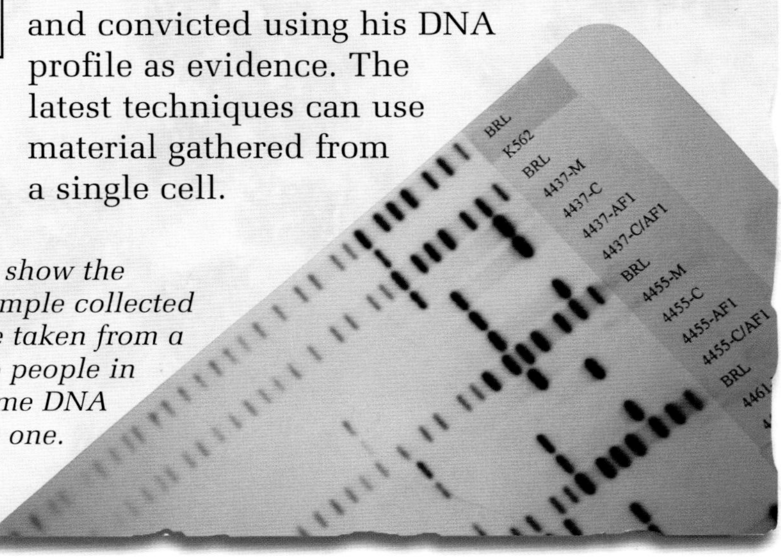

A DNA chart, marked to show the similarities between a sample collected at a crime scene and one taken from a suspect. The odds of two people in the U.S.A. having the same DNA are about 300,000,000 to one.

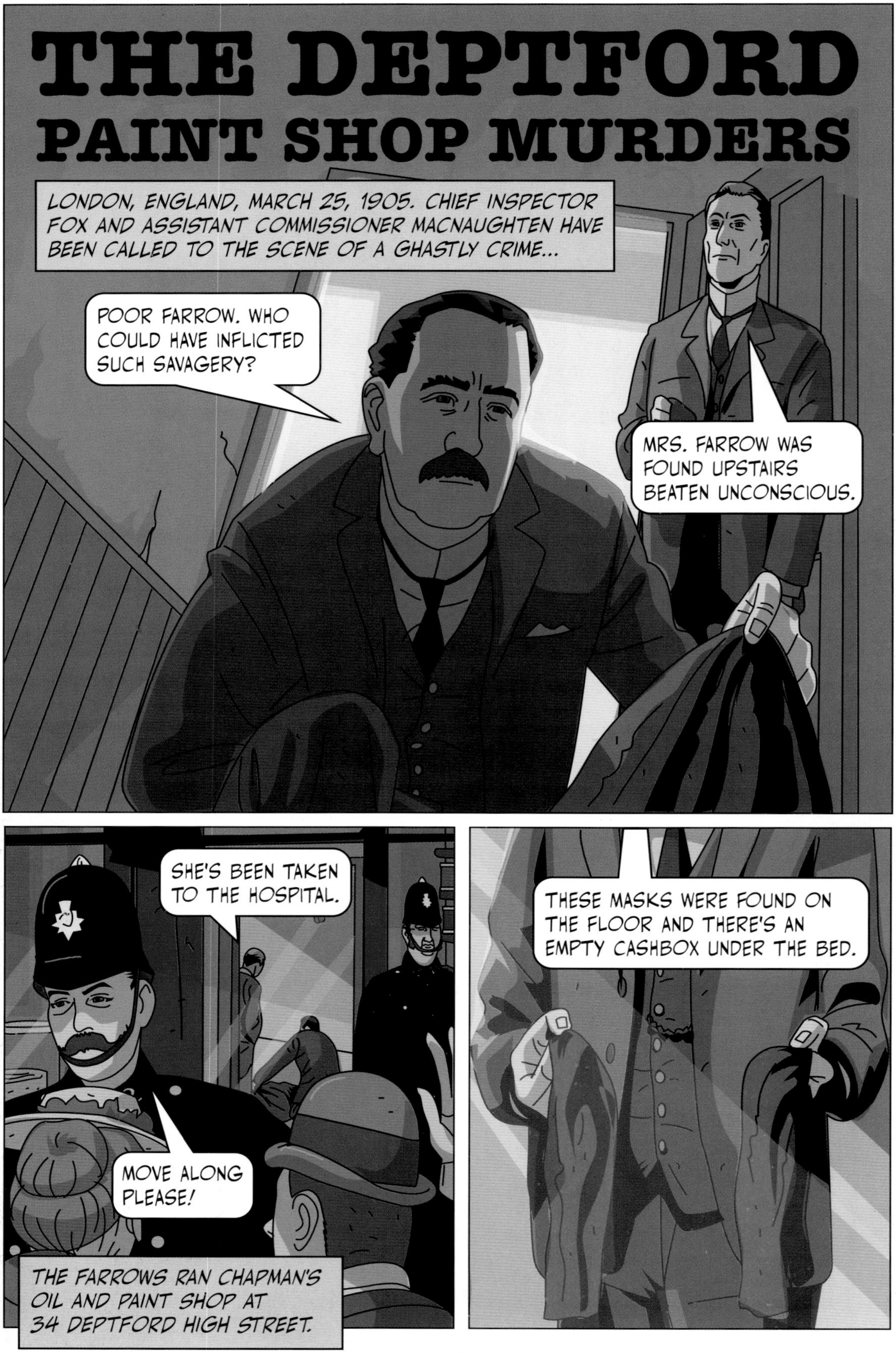
THE DEPTFORD PAINT SHOP MURDERS
LONDON, ENGLAND, MARCH 25, 1905. CHIEF INSPECTOR FOX AND ASSISTANT COMMISSIONER MACNAUGHTEN HAVE BEEN CALLED TO THE SCENE OF A GHASTLY CRIME...
POOR FARROW. WHO COULD HAVE INFLICTED SUCH SAVAGERY?
MRS. FARROW WAS FOUND UPSTAIRS BEATEN UNCONSCIOUS.
SHE'S BEEN TAKEN TO THE HOSPITAL.
MOVE ALONG PLEASE!
THE FARROWS RAN CHAPMAN'S OIL AND PAINT SHOP AT 34 DEPTFORD HIGH STREET.
THESE MASKS WERE FOUND ON THE FLOOR AND THERE'S AN EMPTY CASHBOX UNDER THE BED.

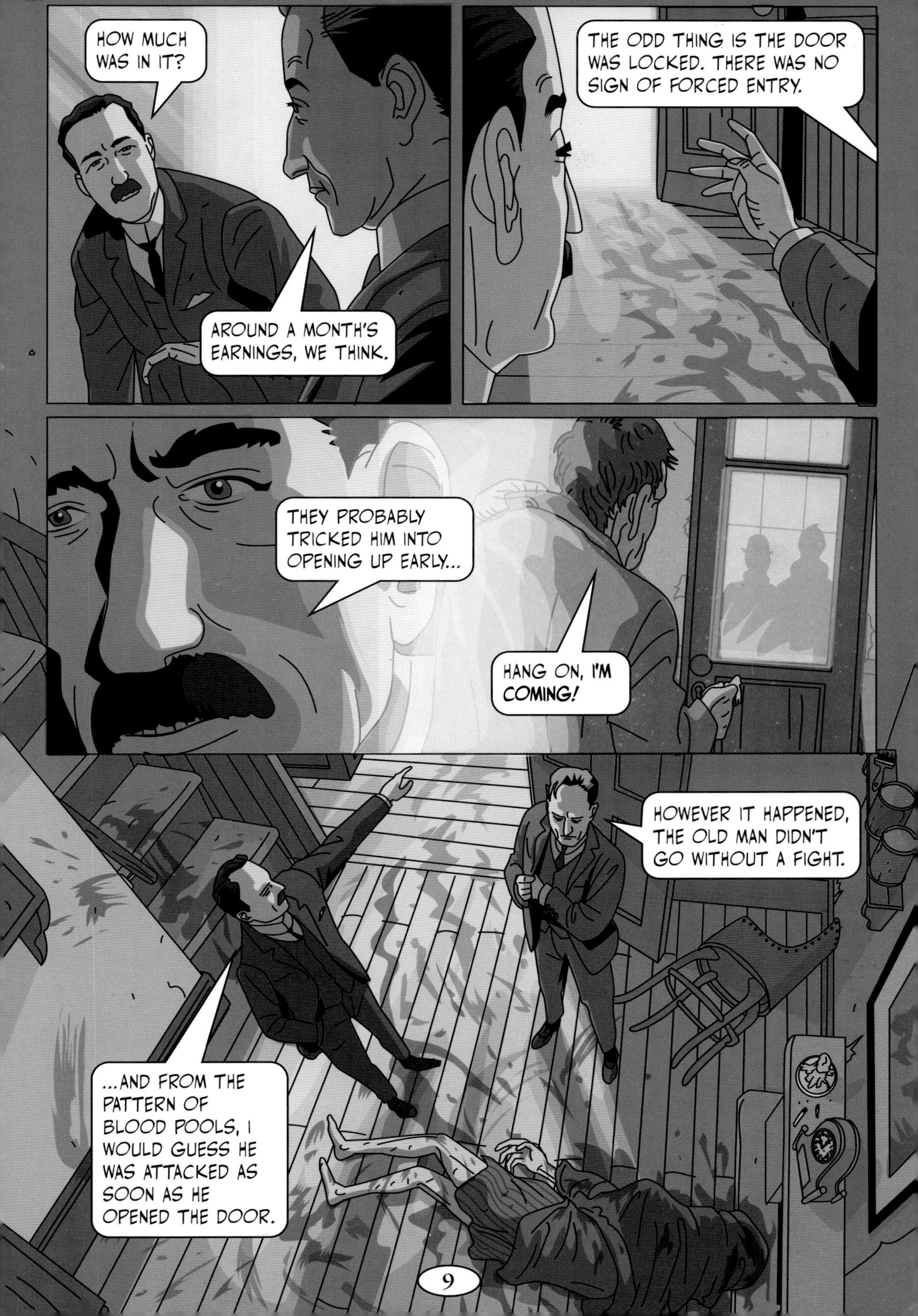
HOW MUCH WAS IN IT?
AROUND A MONTH'S EARNINGS, WE THINK.
THE ODD THING IS THE DOOR WAS LOCKED. THERE WAS NO SIGN OF FORCED ENTRY.
THEY PROBABLY TRICKED HIM INTO OPENING UP EARLY...
HANG ON, I'M COMING!
HOWEVER IT HAPPENED, THE OLD MAN DIDN'T GO WITHOUT A FIGHT.
...AND FROM THE PATTERN OF BLOOD POOLS, I WOULD GUESS HE WAS ATTACKED AS SOON AS HE OPENED THE DOOR.

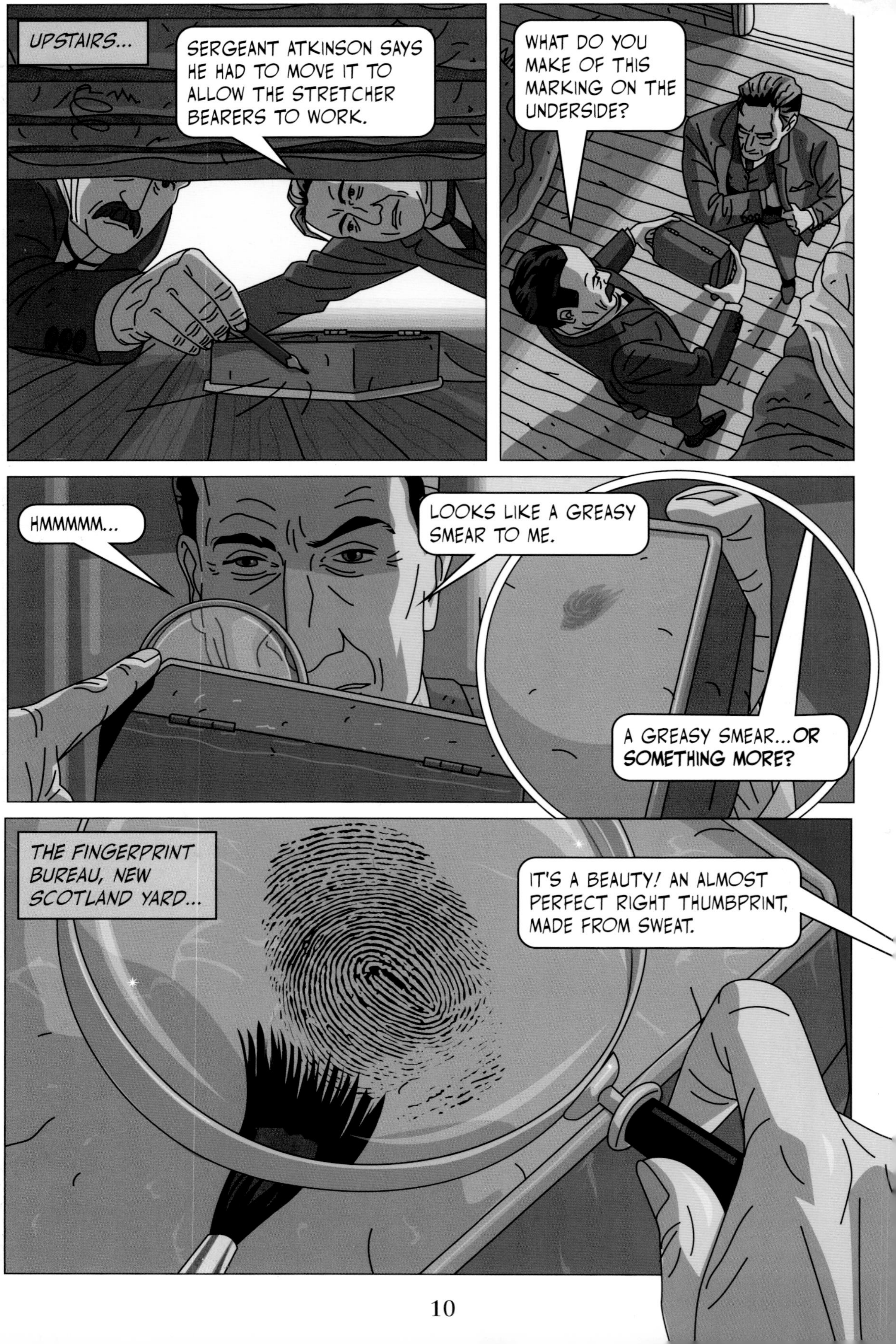
UPSTAIRS...
SERGEANT ATKINSON SAYS HE HAD TO MOVE IT TO ALLOW THE STRETCHER BEARERS TO WORK.
WHAT DO YOU MAKE OF THIS MARKING ON THE UNDERSIDE?
HMMMMM...
LOOKS LIKE A GREASY SMEAR TO ME.
A GREASY SMEAR...OR SOMETHING MORE?
THE FINGERPRINT BUREAU, NEW SCOTLAND YARD...
IT'S A BEAUTY! AN ALMOST PERFECT RIGHT THUMBPRINT, MADE FROM SWEAT.

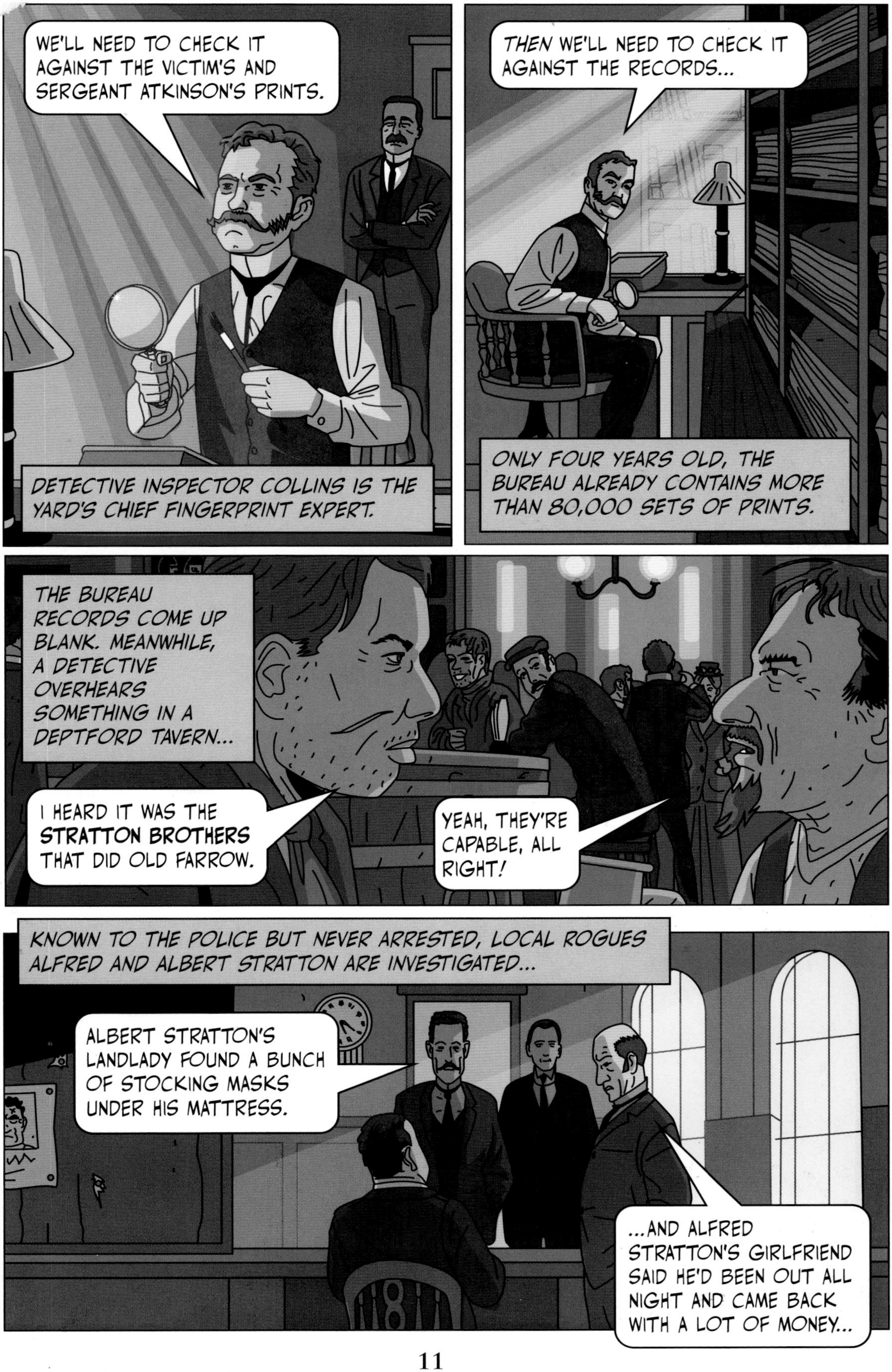
WE'LL NEED TO CHECK IT AGAINST THE VICTIM'S AND SERGEANT ATKINSON'S PRINTS.
DETECTIVE INSPECTOR COLLINS IS THE YARD'S CHIEF FINGERPRINT EXPERT.
THEN WE'LL NEED TO CHECK IT AGAINST THE RECORDS...
ONLY FOUR YEARS OLD, THE BUREAU ALREADY CONTAINS MORE THAN 80,000 SETS OF PRINTS.
THE BUREAU RECORDS COME UP BLANK. MEANWHILE, A DETECTIVE OVERHEARS SOMETHING IN A DEPTFORD TAVERN...
I HEARD IT WAS THE **STRATTON BROTHERS** THAT DID OLD FARROW.
YEAH, THEY'RE CAPABLE, ALL RIGHT!
KNOWN TO THE POLICE BUT NEVER ARRESTED, LOCAL ROGUES ALFRED AND ALBERT STRATTON ARE INVESTIGATED...
ALBERT STRATTON'S LANDLADY FOUND A BUNCH OF STOCKING MASKS UNDER HIS MATTRESS.
...AND ALFRED STRATTON'S GIRLFRIEND SAID HE'D BEEN OUT ALL NIGHT AND CAME BACK WITH A LOT OF MONEY...

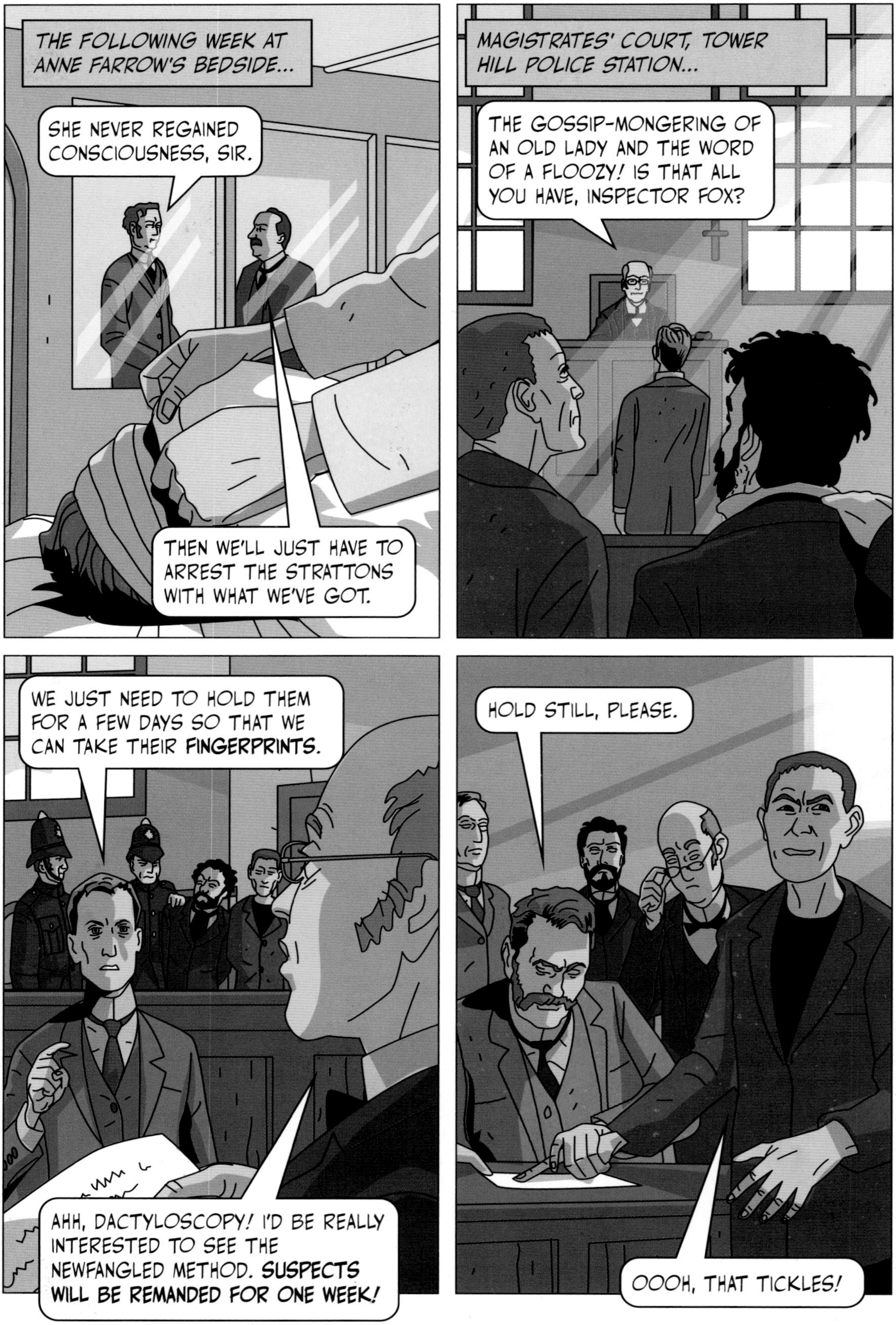
THE FOLLOWING WEEK AT ANNE FARROW'S BEDSIDE...
SHE NEVER REGAINED CONSCIOUSNESS, SIR.
THEN WE'LL JUST HAVE TO ARREST THE STRATTONS WITH WHAT WE'VE GOT.
MAGISTRATES' COURT, TOWER HILL POLICE STATION...
THE GOSSIP-MONGERING OF AN OLD LADY AND THE WORD OF A FLOOZY! IS THAT ALL YOU HAVE, INSPECTOR FOX?
WE JUST NEED TO HOLD THEM FOR A FEW DAYS SO THAT WE CAN TAKE THEIR **FINGERPRINTS**.
AHH, DACTYLOSCOPY! I'D BE REALLY INTERESTED TO SEE THE NEWFANGLED METHOD. **SUSPECTS WILL BE REMANDED FOR ONE WEEK!**
HOLD STILL, PLEASE.
OOOH, THAT TICKLES!

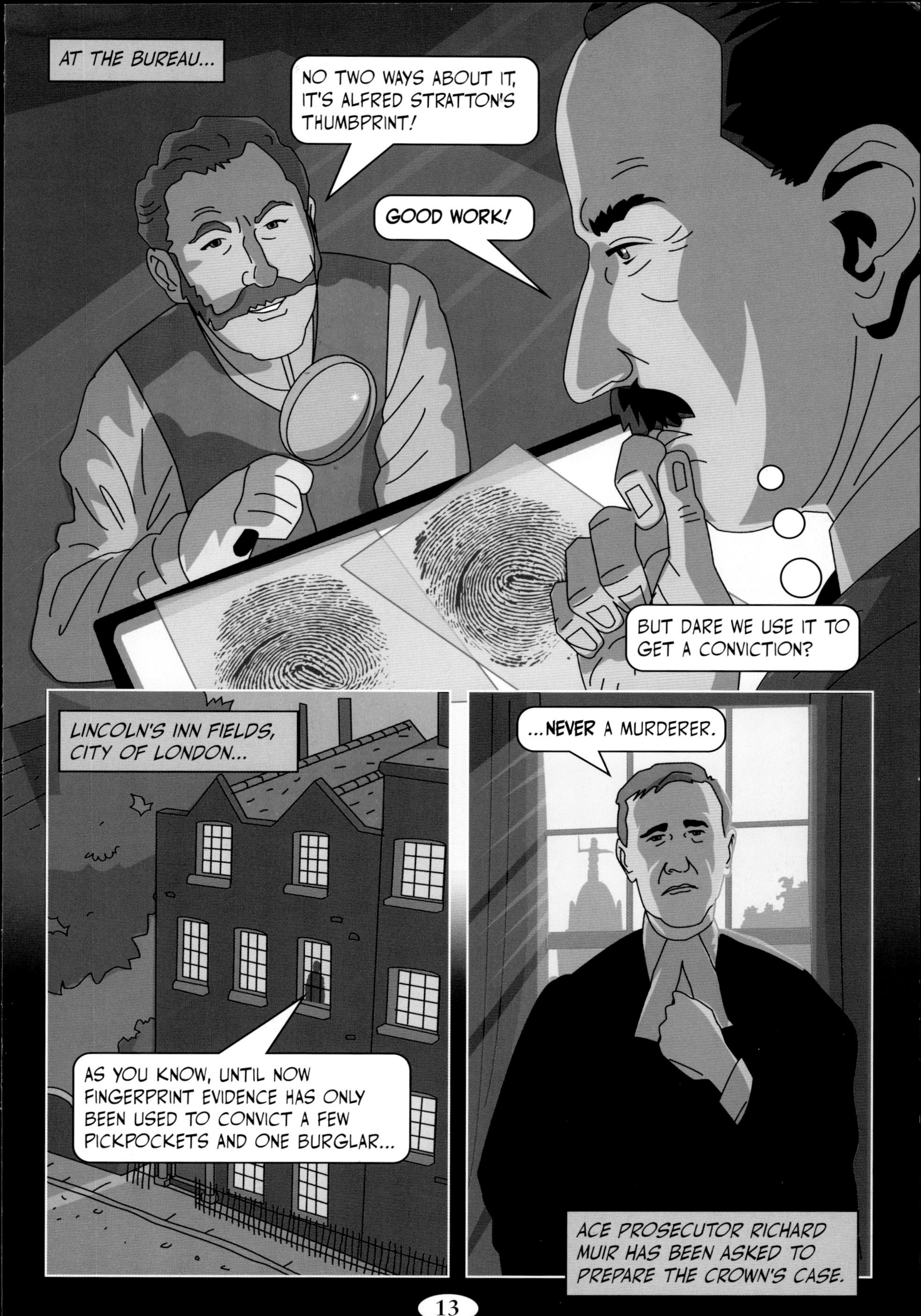

AT THE BUREAU...
NO TWO WAYS ABOUT IT, IT'S ALFRED STRATTON'S THUMBPRINT!
GOOD WORK!
BUT DARE WE USE IT TO GET A CONVICTION?
LINCOLN'S INN FIELDS, CITY OF LONDON...
AS YOU KNOW, UNTIL NOW FINGERPRINT EVIDENCE HAS ONLY BEEN USED TO CONVICT A FEW PICKPOCKETS AND ONE BURGLAR...
...**NEVER** A MURDERER.
ACE PROSECUTOR RICHARD MUIR HAS BEEN ASKED TO PREPARE THE CROWN'S CASE.

BUT ALL WE HAVE IS CIRCUMSTANTIAL EVIDENCE AND WITNESSES WHO CLAIM TO HAVE SEEN THE STRATTONS LEAVING THE SHOP...

...ONE OF WHOM, A MILKMAN, SAYS HE NOW CAN'T BE SURE!

ALL RIGHT, BUT BE AWARE THAT THE WHOLE *METHOD* OF FINGERPRINTING WILL ALSO BE ON TRIAL ALONG WITH THE DEFENDANTS.

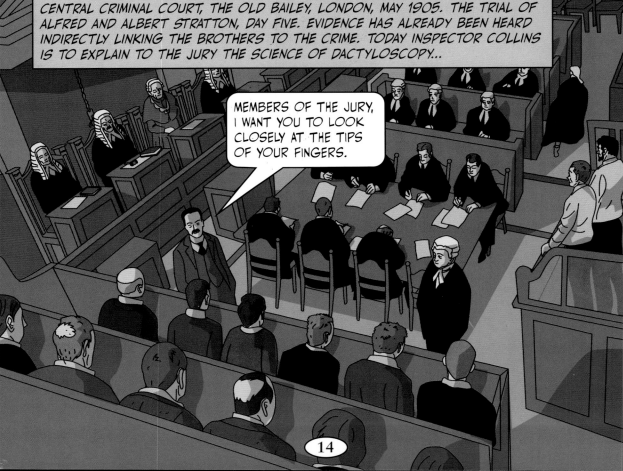

CENTRAL CRIMINAL COURT, THE OLD BAILEY, LONDON, MAY 1905. THE TRIAL OF ALFRED AND ALBERT STRATTON, DAY FIVE. EVIDENCE HAS ALREADY BEEN HEARD INDIRECTLY LINKING THE BROTHERS TO THE CRIME. TODAY INSPECTOR COLLINS IS TO EXPLAIN TO THE JURY THE SCIENCE OF DACTYLOSCOPY...

MEMBERS OF THE JURY, I WANT YOU TO LOOK CLOSELY AT THE TIPS OF YOUR FINGERS.

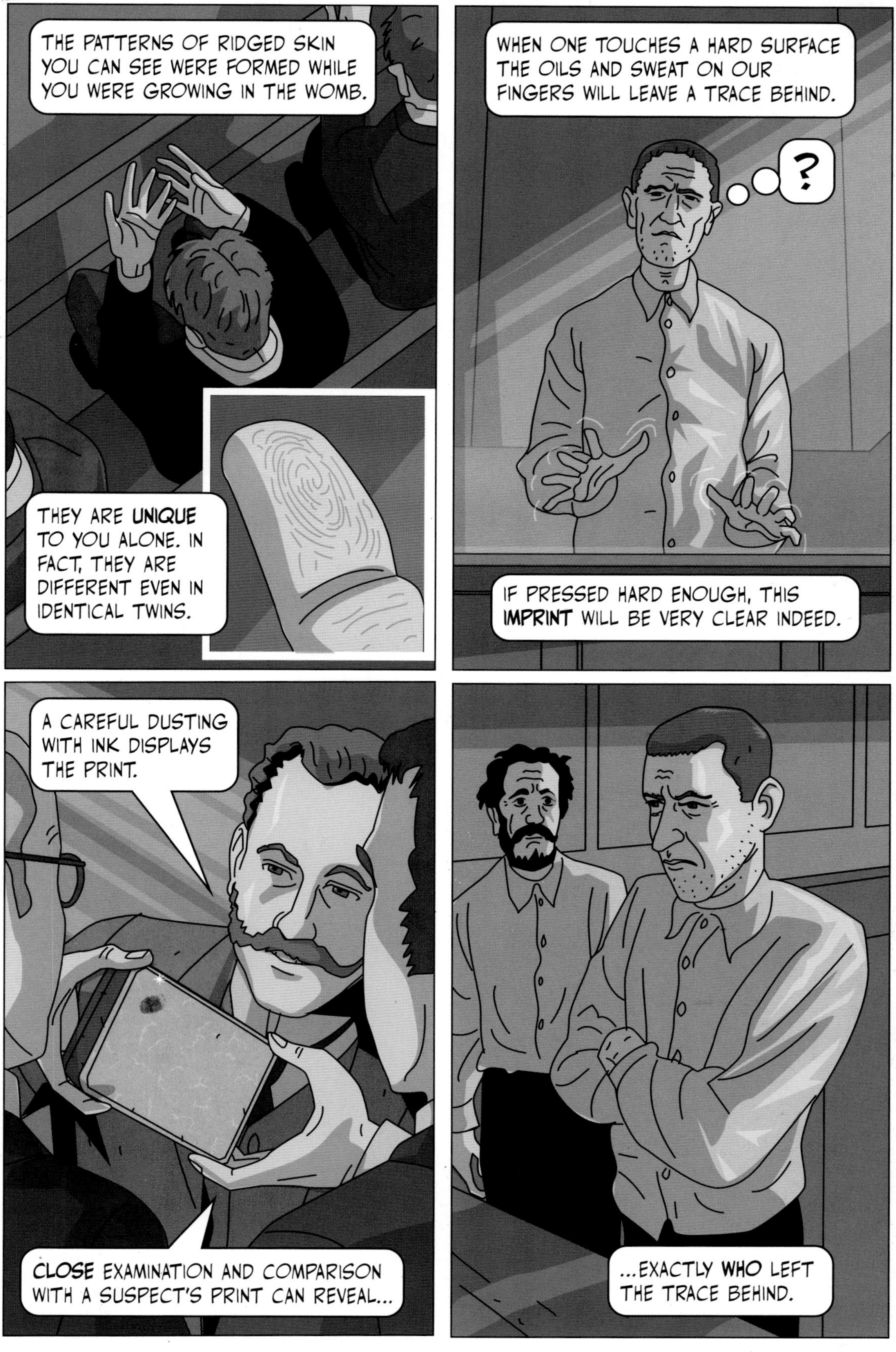
THE PATTERNS OF RIDGED SKIN YOU CAN SEE WERE FORMED WHILE YOU WERE GROWING IN THE WOMB.
THEY ARE **UNIQUE** TO YOU ALONE. IN FACT, THEY ARE DIFFERENT EVEN IN IDENTICAL TWINS.
WHEN ONE TOUCHES A HARD SURFACE THE OILS AND SWEAT ON OUR FINGERS WILL LEAVE A TRACE BEHIND.
?
IF PRESSED HARD ENOUGH, THIS **IMPRINT** WILL BE VERY CLEAR INDEED.
A CAREFUL DUSTING WITH INK DISPLAYS THE PRINT.
CLOSE EXAMINATION AND COMPARISON WITH A SUSPECT'S PRINT CAN REVEAL...
...EXACTLY **WHO** LEFT THE TRACE BEHIND.

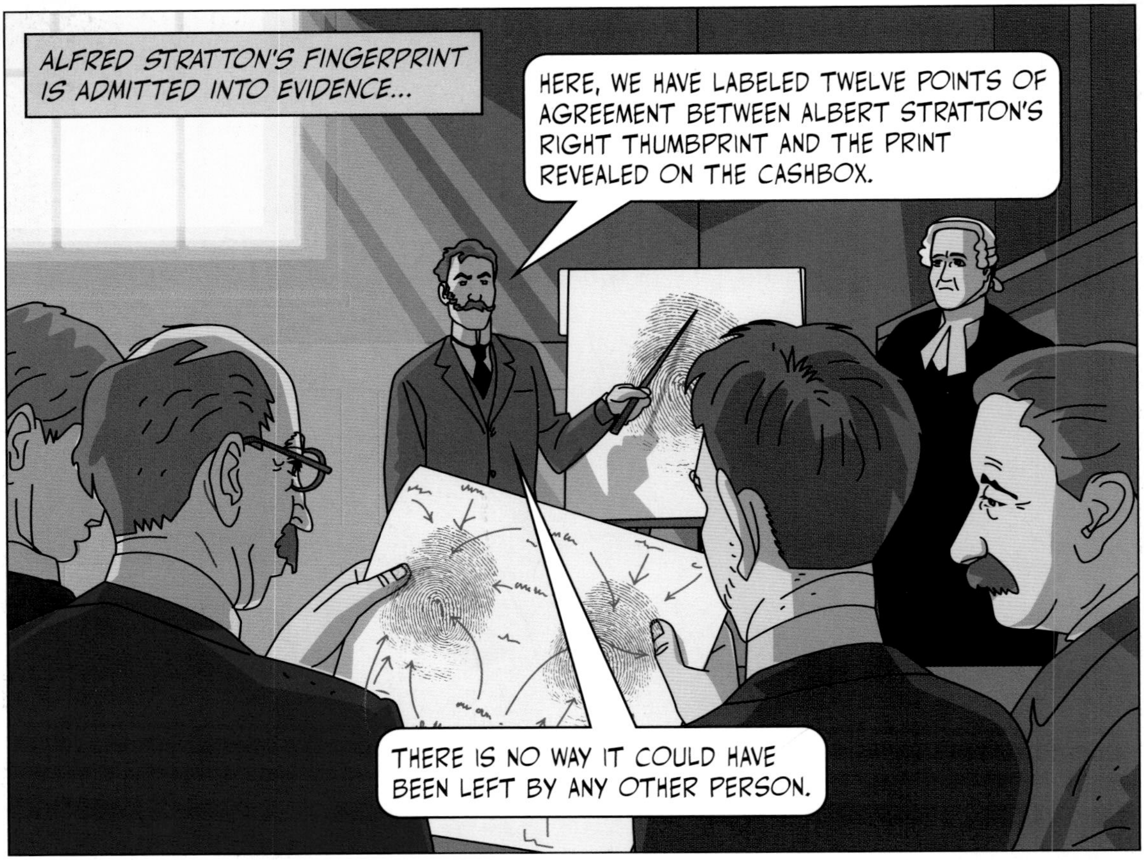
ALFRED STRATTON'S FINGERPRINT IS ADMITTED INTO EVIDENCE...
HERE, WE HAVE LABELED TWELVE POINTS OF AGREEMENT BETWEEN ALBERT STRATTON'S RIGHT THUMBPRINT AND THE PRINT REVEALED ON THE CASHBOX.
THERE IS NO WAY IT COULD HAVE BEEN LEFT BY ANY OTHER PERSON.

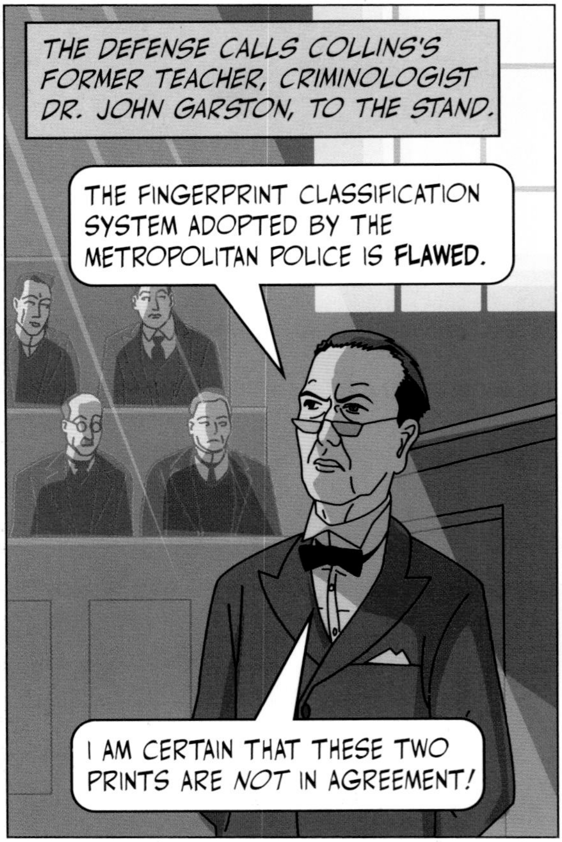
THE DEFENSE CALLS COLLINS'S FORMER TEACHER, CRIMINOLOGIST DR. JOHN GARSTON, TO THE STAND.
THE FINGERPRINT CLASSIFICATION SYSTEM ADOPTED BY THE METROPOLITAN POLICE IS **FLAWED.**
I AM CERTAIN THAT THESE TWO PRINTS ARE *NOT* IN AGREEMENT!

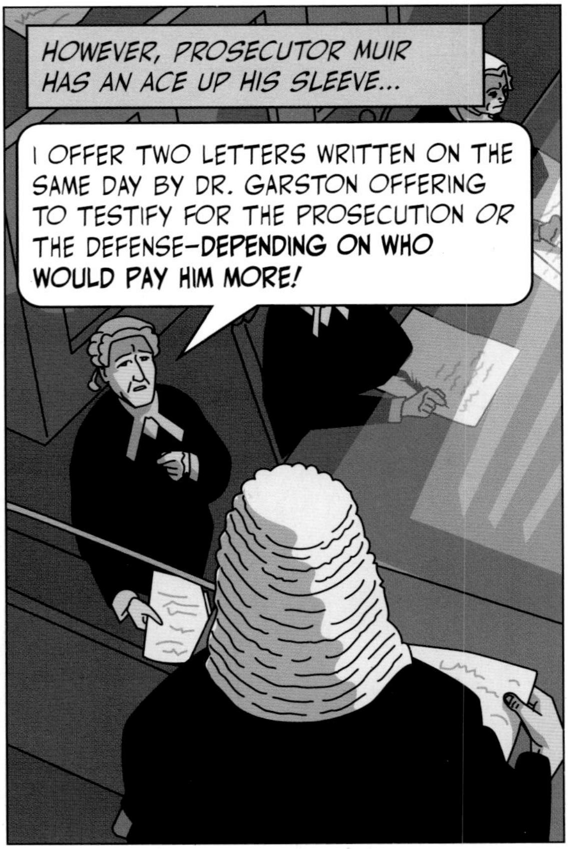
HOWEVER, PROSECUTOR MUIR HAS AN ACE UP HIS SLEEVE...
I OFFER TWO LETTERS WRITTEN ON THE SAME DAY BY DR. GARSTON OFFERING TO TESTIFY FOR THE PROSECUTION *OR* THE DEFENSE—**DEPENDING ON WHO WOULD PAY HIM MORE!**

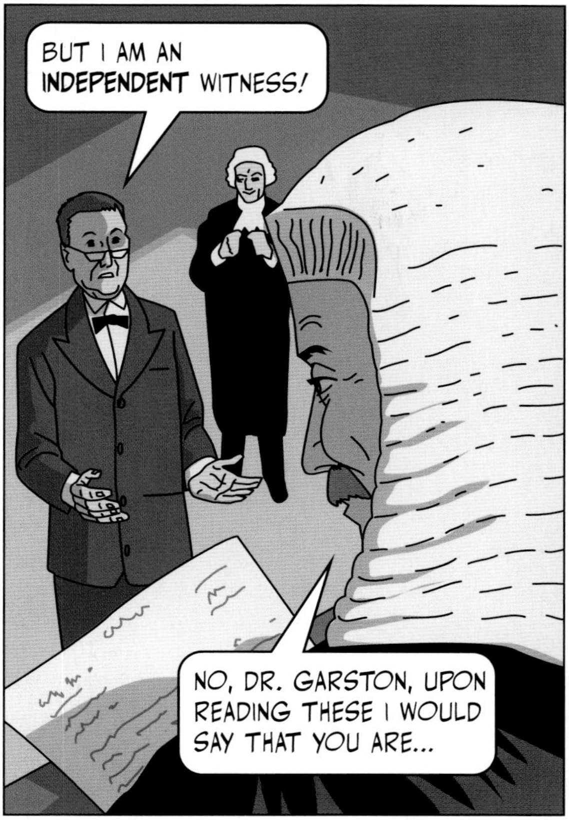
BUT I AM AN INDEPENDENT WITNESS!
NO, DR. GARSTON, UPON READING THESE I WOULD SAY THAT YOU ARE...

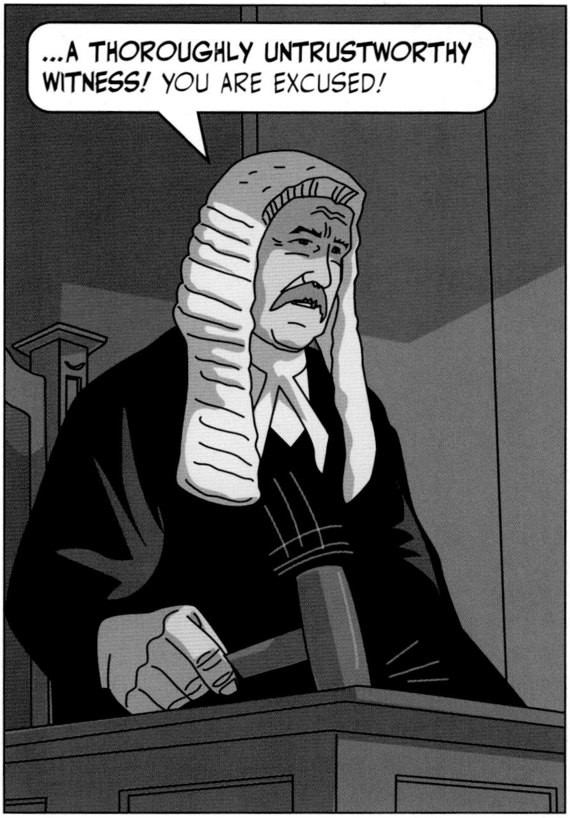
...A THOROUGHLY UNTRUSTWORTHY WITNESS! YOU ARE EXCUSED!

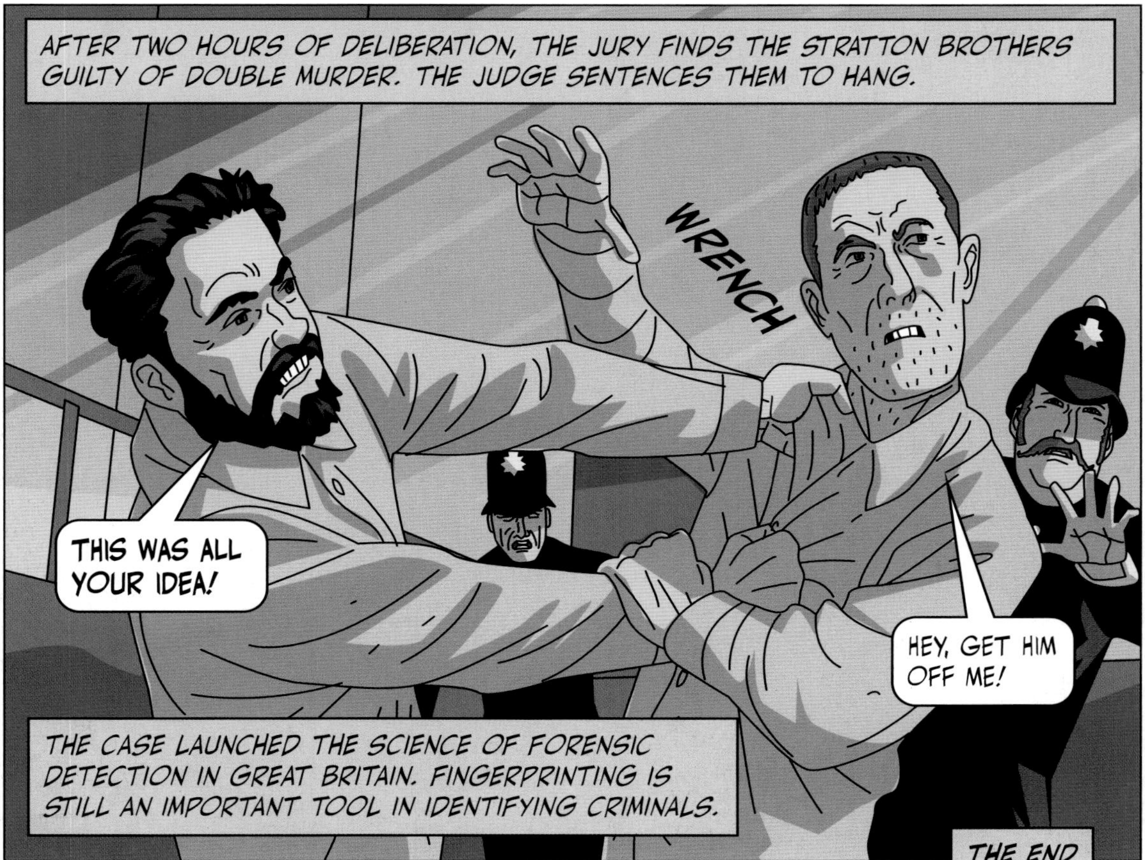
AFTER TWO HOURS OF DELIBERATION, THE JURY FINDS THE STRATTON BROTHERS GUILTY OF DOUBLE MURDER. THE JUDGE SENTENCES THEM TO HANG.
WRENCH
THIS WAS ALL YOUR IDEA!
HEY, GET HIM OFF ME!
THE CASE LAUNCHED THE SCIENCE OF FORENSIC DETECTION IN GREAT BRITAIN. FINGERPRINTING IS STILL AN IMPORTANT TOOL IN IDENTIFYING CRIMINALS.
THE END

THE CORPSE IN THE COURTYARD

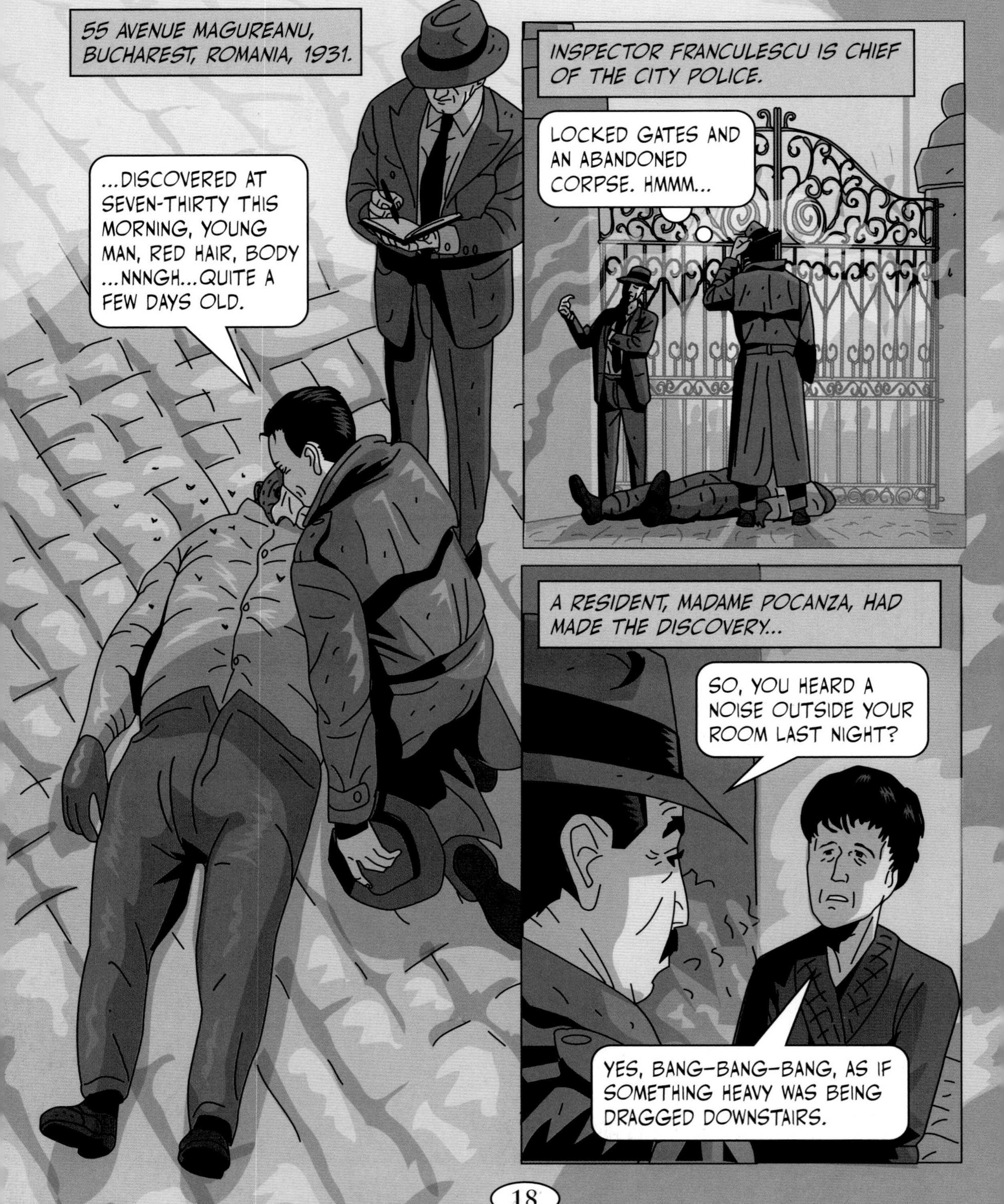

55 AVENUE MAGUREANU, BUCHAREST, ROMANIA, 1931.
...DISCOVERED AT SEVEN-THIRTY THIS MORNING, YOUNG MAN, RED HAIR, BODY ...NNNGH...QUITE A FEW DAYS OLD.
INSPECTOR FRANCULESCU IS CHIEF OF THE CITY POLICE.
LOCKED GATES AND AN ABANDONED CORPSE. HMMM...
A RESIDENT, MADAME POCANZA, HAD MADE THE DISCOVERY...
SO, YOU HEARD A NOISE OUTSIDE YOUR ROOM LAST NIGHT?
YES, BANG-BANG-BANG, AS IF SOMETHING HEAVY WAS BEING DRAGGED DOWNSTAIRS.

I CALLED OUT BUT NO ONE REPLIED, SO I PAID IT NO ATTENTION. THEN THIS MORNING—THIS!

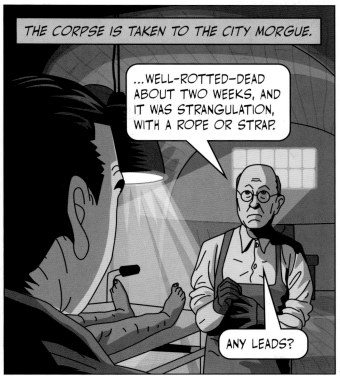

THE CORPSE IS TAKEN TO THE CITY MORGUE.

...WELL-ROTTED—DEAD ABOUT TWO WEEKS, AND IT WAS STRANGULATION, WITH A ROPE OR STRAP.

ANY LEADS?

NOT YET, BUT WE'VE RULED OUT THE TENANTS—THEY ALL KNEW WHEN THE GATES WOULD BE LOCKED.

MEANWHILE, FRANCULESCU'S MEN HAVE CONDUCTED A SEARCH...

NOTHING! NO LINGERING STENCH OR STAINS. THE BODY HASN'T BEEN KEPT HERE.

NOT IN THE BUILDING, MAYBE, BUT WHAT ABOUT IN THE ROOF SPACE?

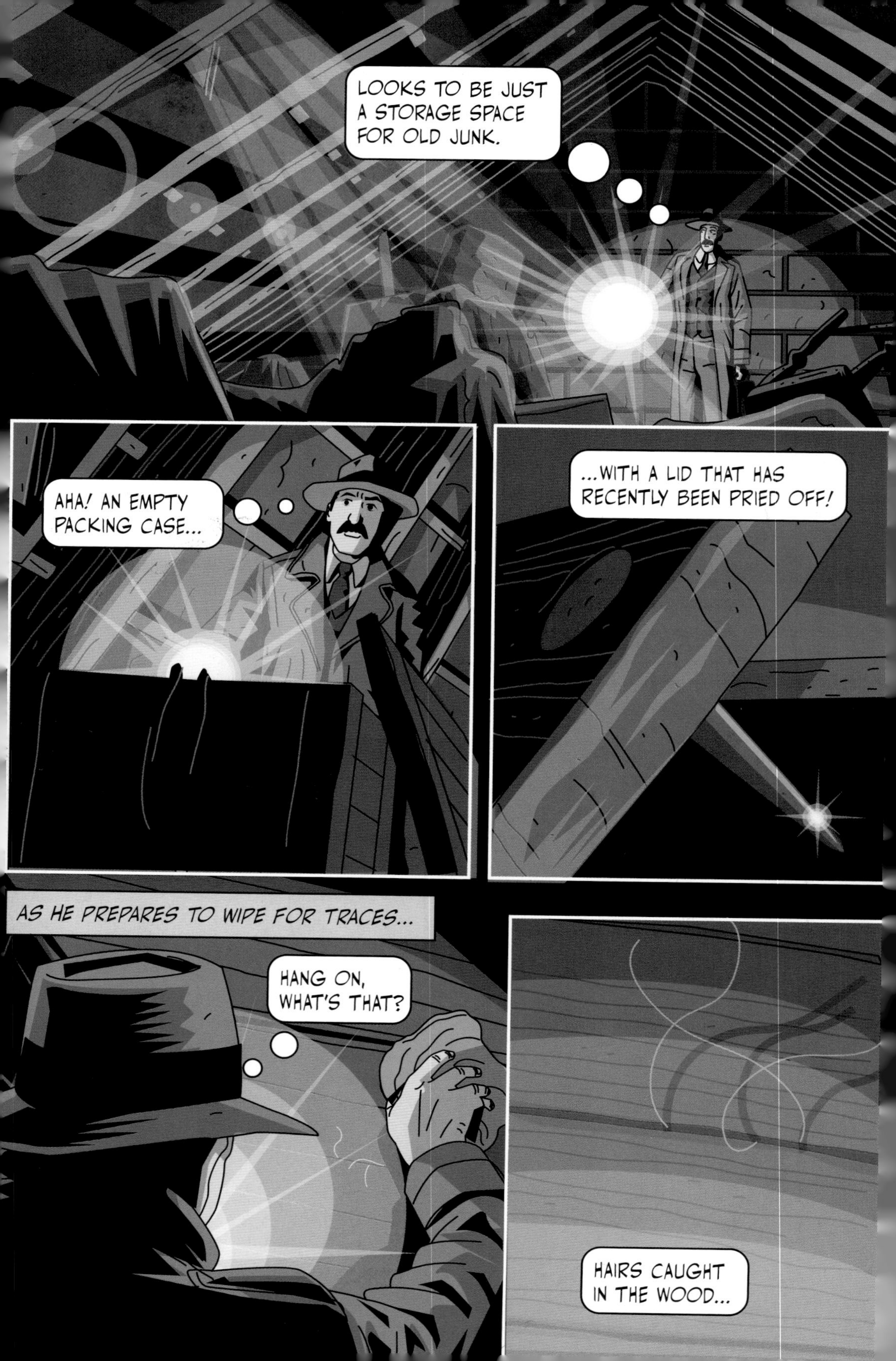
LOOKS TO BE JUST A STORAGE SPACE FOR OLD JUNK.
AHA! AN EMPTY PACKING CASE...
...WITH A LID THAT HAS RECENTLY BEEN PRIED OFF!
AS HE PREPARES TO WIPE FOR TRACES...
HANG ON, WHAT'S THAT?
HAIRS CAUGHT IN THE WOOD...

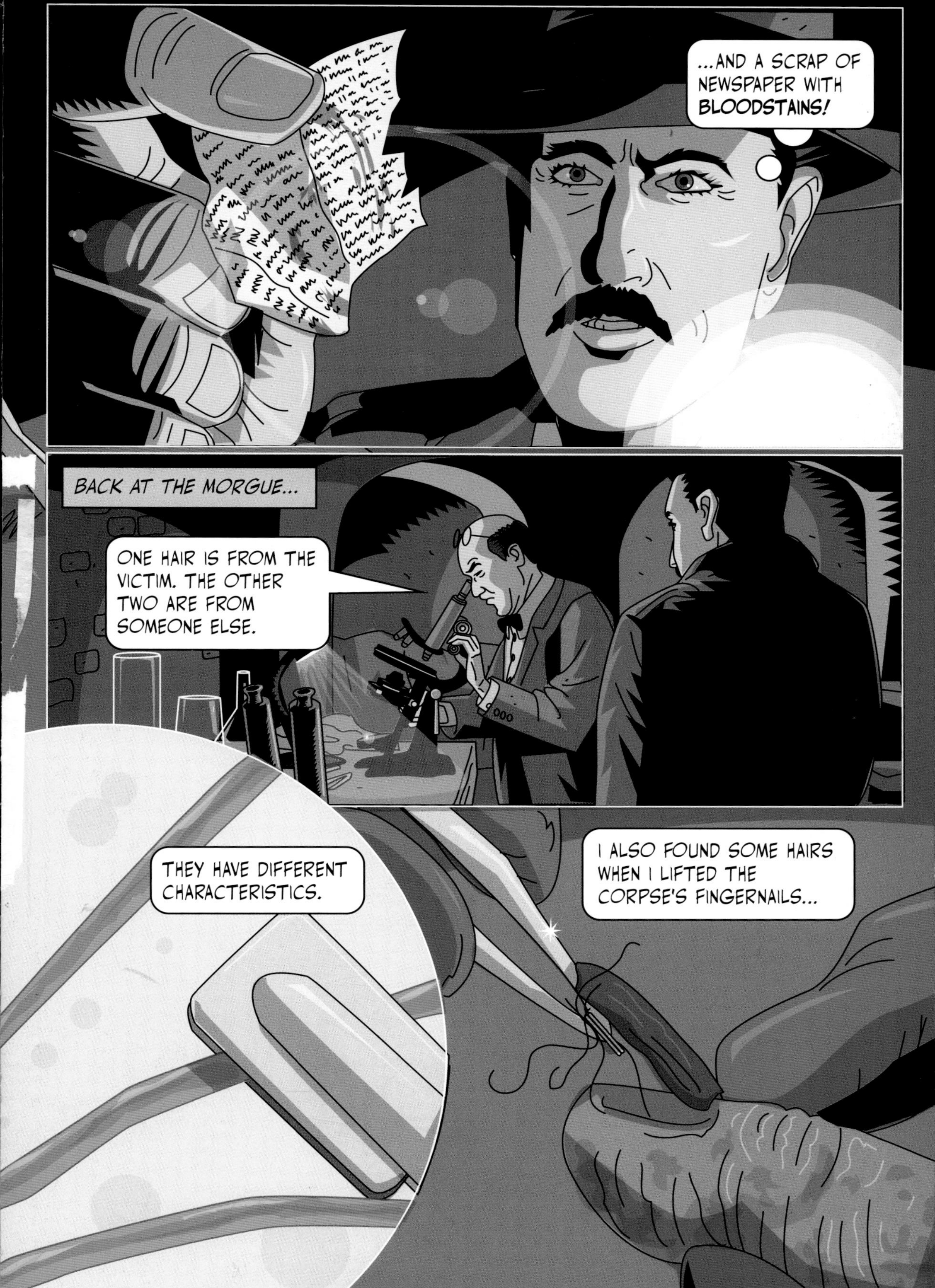

...AND A SCRAP OF NEWSPAPER WITH BLOODSTAINS!
BACK AT THE MORGUE...
ONE HAIR IS FROM THE VICTIM. THE OTHER TWO ARE FROM SOMEONE ELSE.
I ALSO FOUND SOME HAIRS WHEN I LIFTED THE CORPSE'S FINGERNAILS...
THEY HAVE DIFFERENT CHARACTERISTICS.

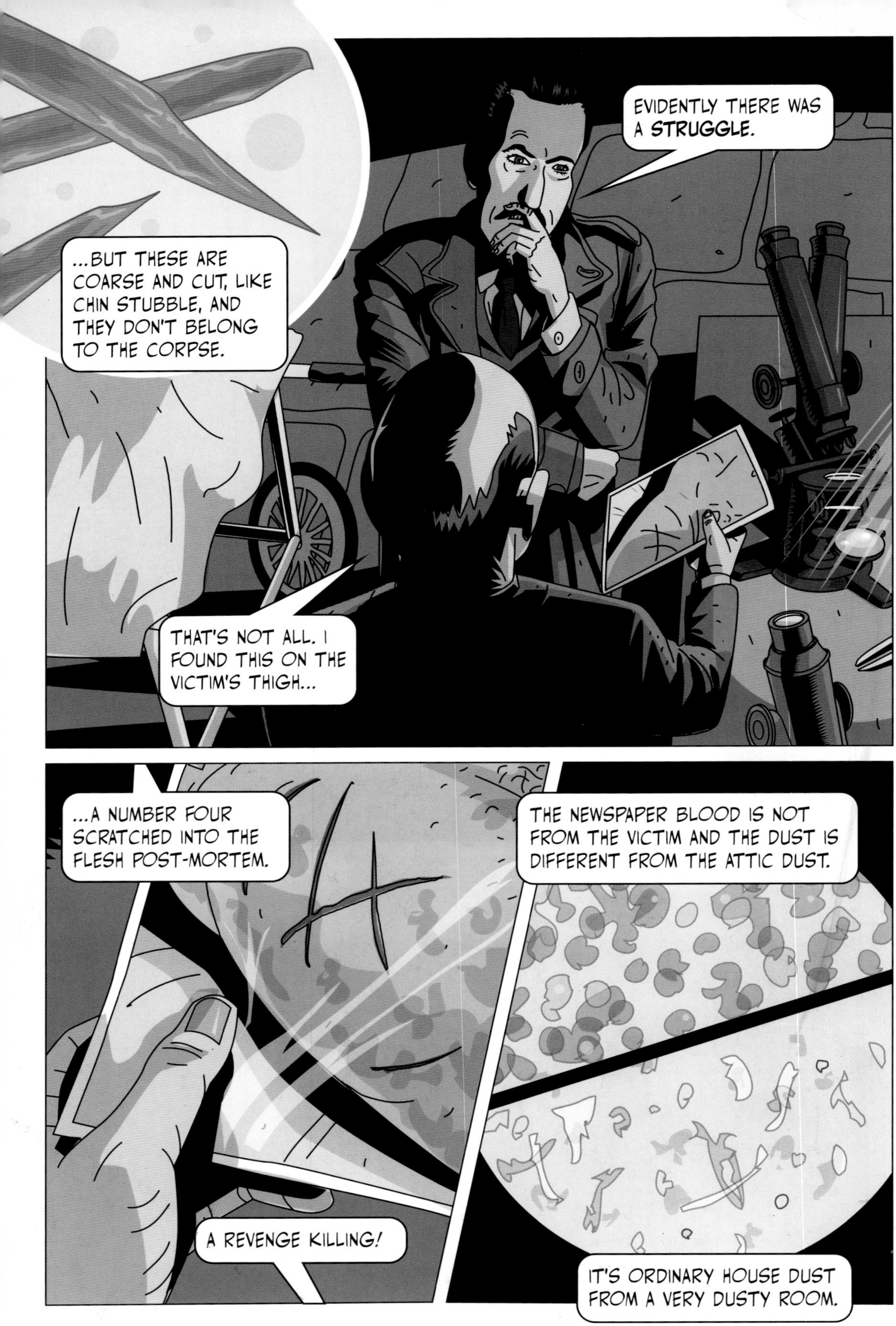
...BUT THESE ARE COARSE AND CUT, LIKE CHIN STUBBLE, AND THEY DON'T BELONG TO THE CORPSE.
EVIDENTLY THERE WAS A **STRUGGLE**.
THAT'S NOT ALL. I FOUND THIS ON THE VICTIM'S THIGH...
...A NUMBER FOUR SCRATCHED INTO THE FLESH POST-MORTEM.
A REVENGE KILLING!
THE NEWSPAPER BLOOD IS NOT FROM THE VICTIM AND THE DUST IS DIFFERENT FROM THE ATTIC DUST.
IT'S ORDINARY HOUSE DUST FROM A VERY DUSTY ROOM.

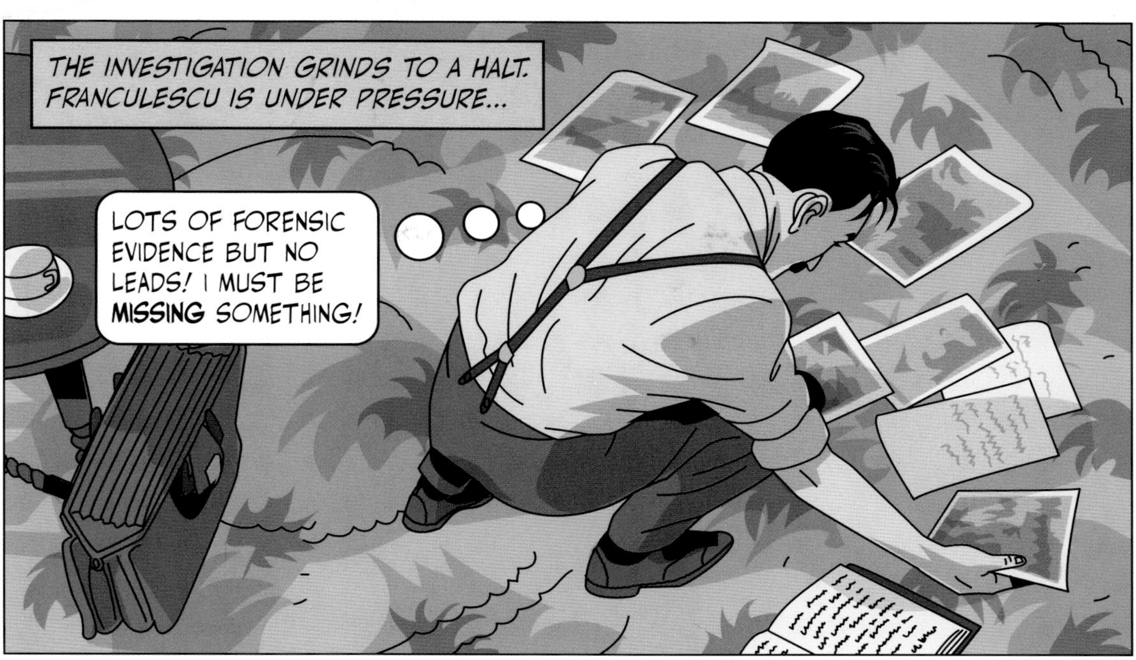
THE INVESTIGATION GRINDS TO A HALT. FRANCULESCU IS UNDER PRESSURE...
LOTS OF FORENSIC EVIDENCE BUT NO LEADS! I MUST BE **MISSING** SOMETHING!

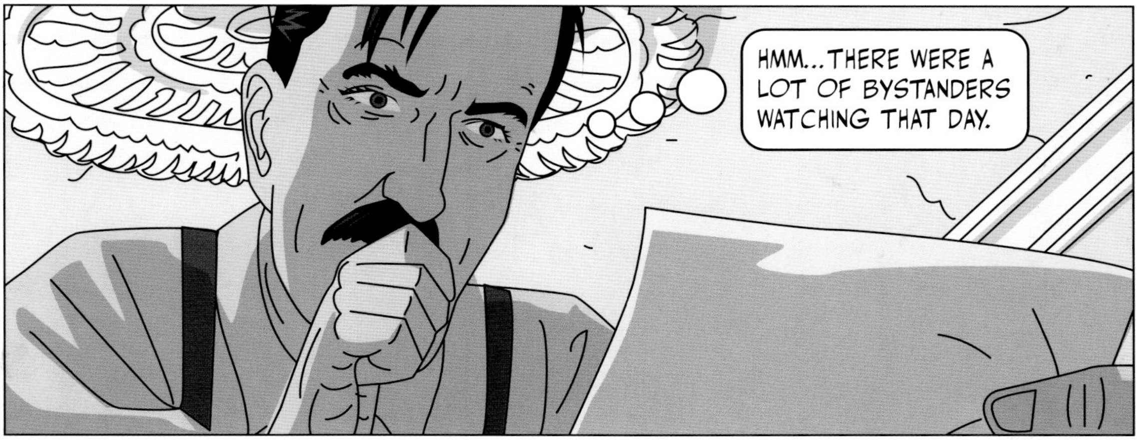
HMM...THERE WERE A LOT OF BYSTANDERS WATCHING THAT DAY.

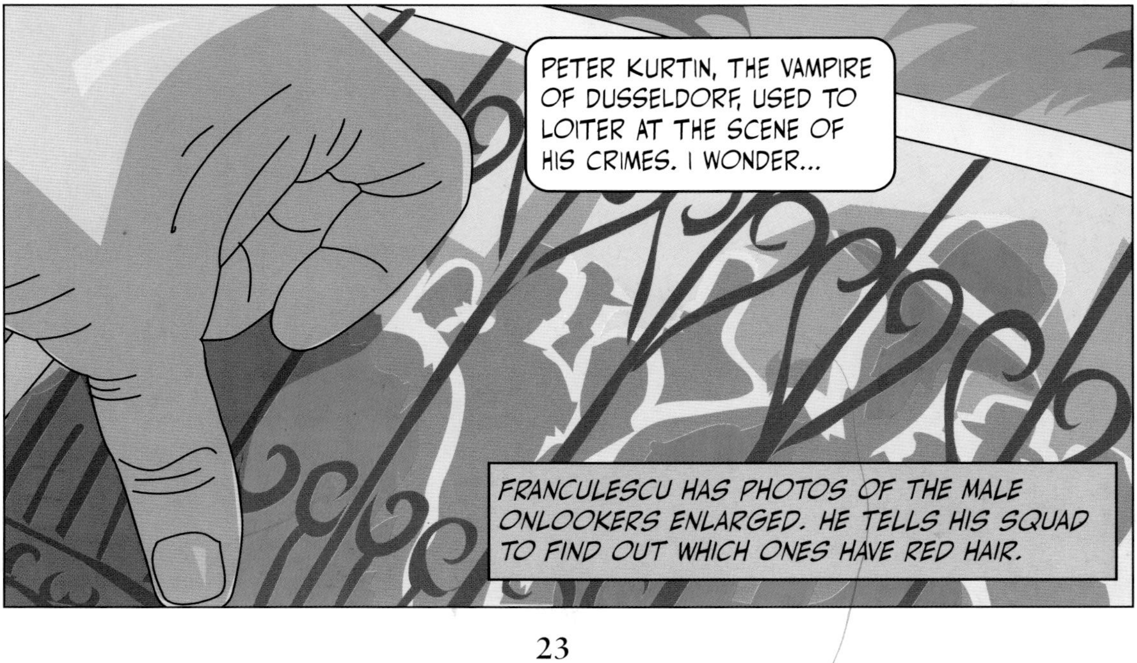
PETER KURTIN, THE VAMPIRE OF DUSSELDORF, USED TO LOITER AT THE SCENE OF HIS CRIMES. I WONDER...
FRANCULESCU HAS PHOTOS OF THE MALE ONLOOKERS ENLARGED. HE TELLS HIS SQUAD TO FIND OUT WHICH ONES HAVE RED HAIR.

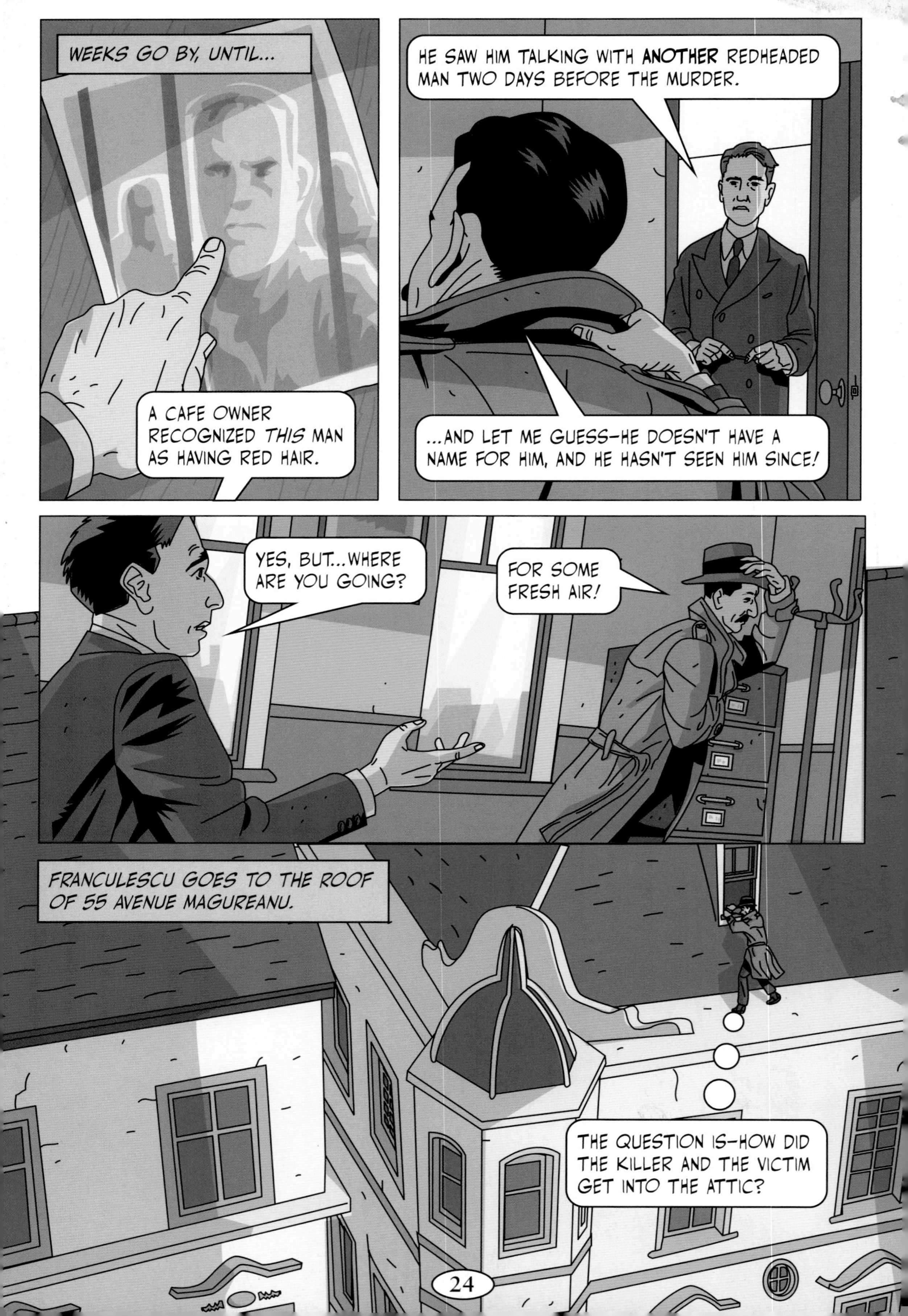
WEEKS GO BY, UNTIL...
A CAFE OWNER RECOGNIZED THIS MAN AS HAVING RED HAIR.
HE SAW HIM TALKING WITH ANOTHER REDHEADED MAN TWO DAYS BEFORE THE MURDER.
...AND LET ME GUESS—HE DOESN'T HAVE A NAME FOR HIM, AND HE HASN'T SEEN HIM SINCE!
YES, BUT...WHERE ARE YOU GOING?
FOR SOME FRESH AIR!
FRANCULESCU GOES TO THE ROOF OF 55 AVENUE MAGUREANU.
THE QUESTION IS—HOW DID THE KILLER AND THE VICTIM GET INTO THE ATTIC?

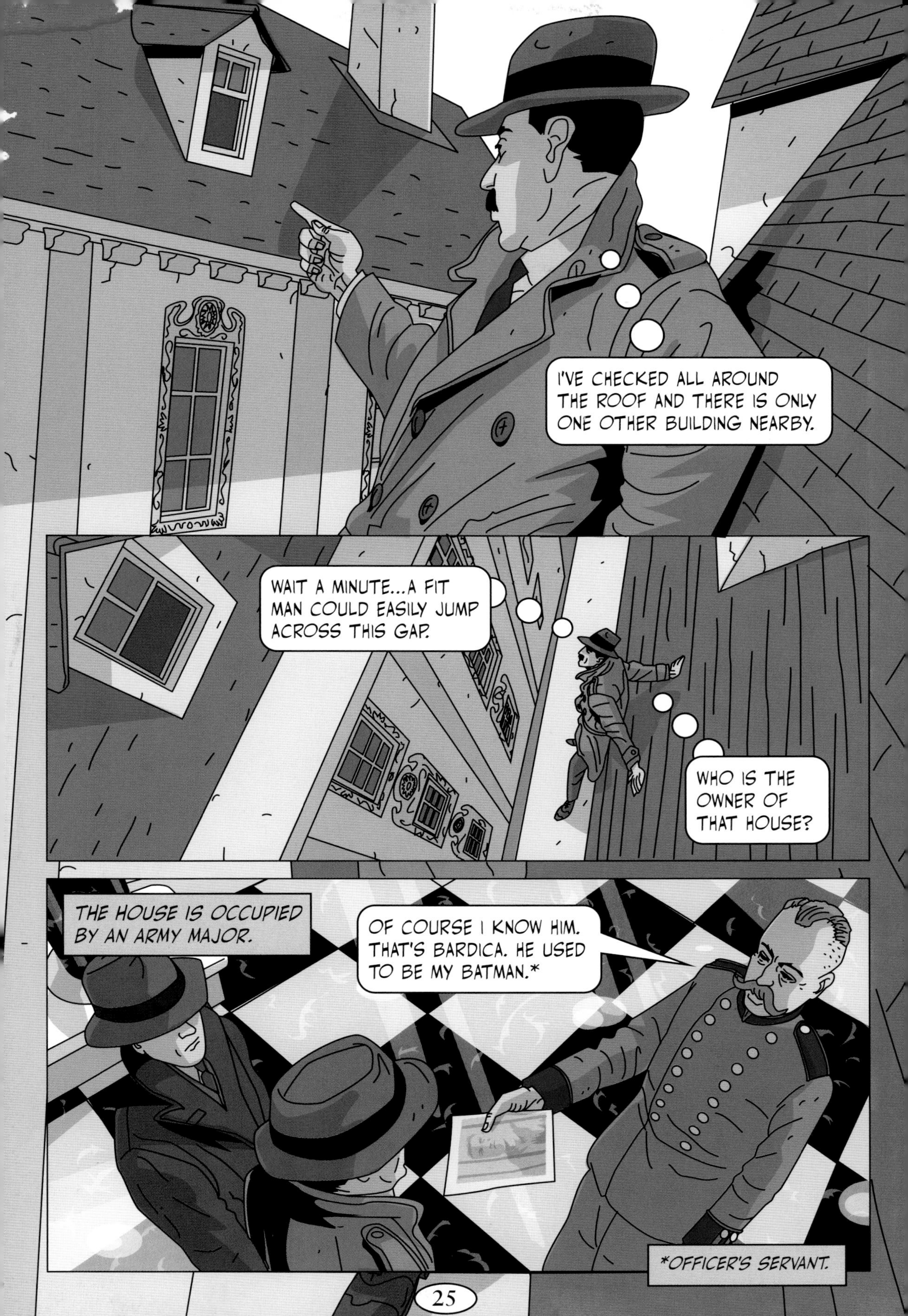
I'VE CHECKED ALL AROUND THE ROOF AND THERE IS ONLY ONE OTHER BUILDING NEARBY.
WAIT A MINUTE...A FIT MAN COULD EASILY JUMP ACROSS THIS GAP.
WHO IS THE OWNER OF THAT HOUSE?
THE HOUSE IS OCCUPIED BY AN ARMY MAJOR.
OF COURSE I KNOW HIM. THAT'S BARDICA. HE USED TO BE MY BATMAN.*
*OFFICER'S SERVANT.

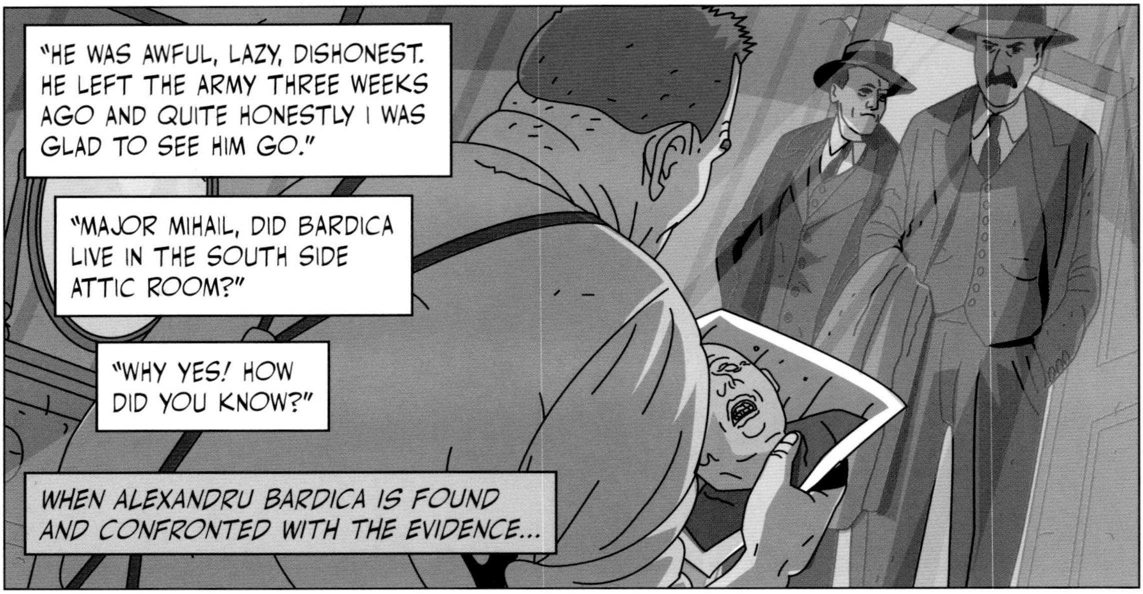
"HE WAS AWFUL, LAZY, DISHONEST. HE LEFT THE ARMY THREE WEEKS AGO AND QUITE HONESTLY I WAS GLAD TO SEE HIM GO."
"MAJOR MIHAIL, DID BARDICA LIVE IN THE SOUTH SIDE ATTIC ROOM?"
"WHY YES! HOW DID YOU KNOW?"
WHEN ALEXANDRU BARDICA IS FOUND AND CONFRONTED WITH THE EVIDENCE...

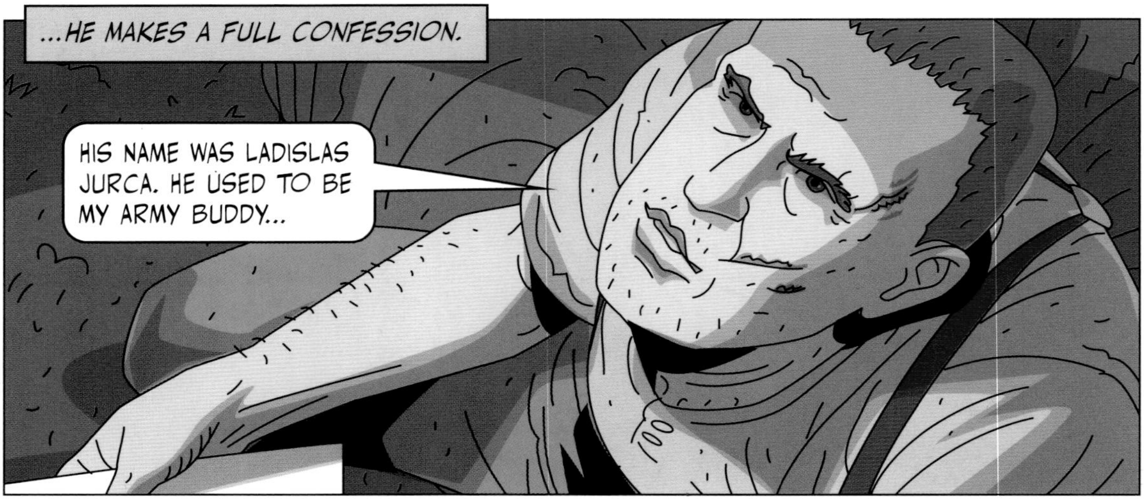
...HE MAKES A FULL CONFESSION.
HIS NAME WAS LADISLAS JURCA. HE USED TO BE MY ARMY BUDDY...

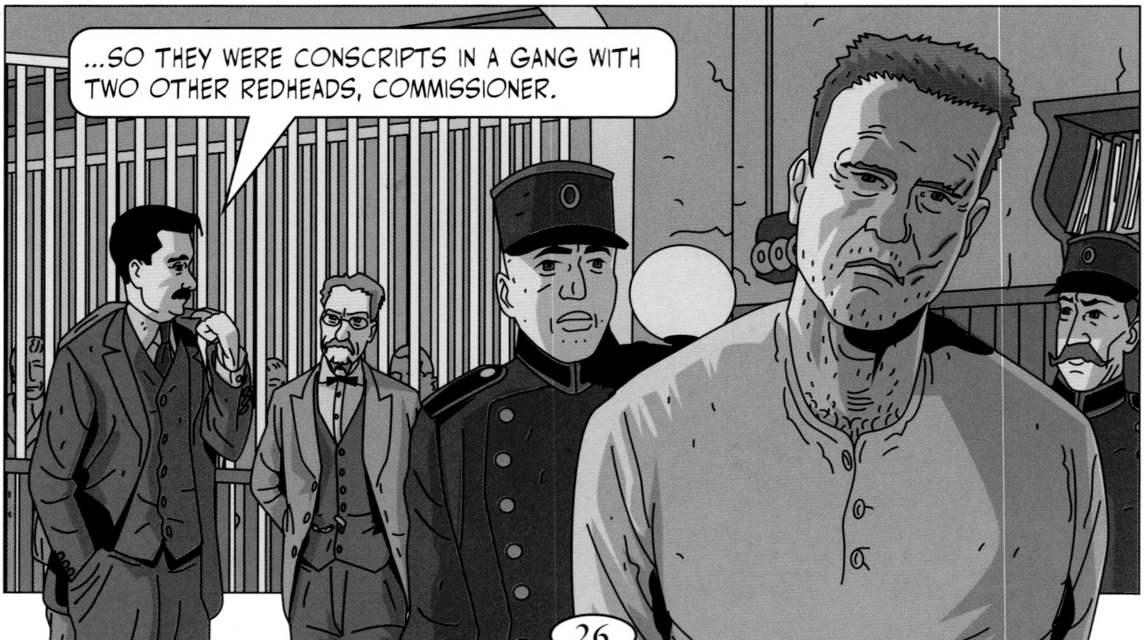
...SO THEY WERE CONSCRIPTS IN A GANG WITH TWO OTHER REDHEADS, COMMISSIONER.

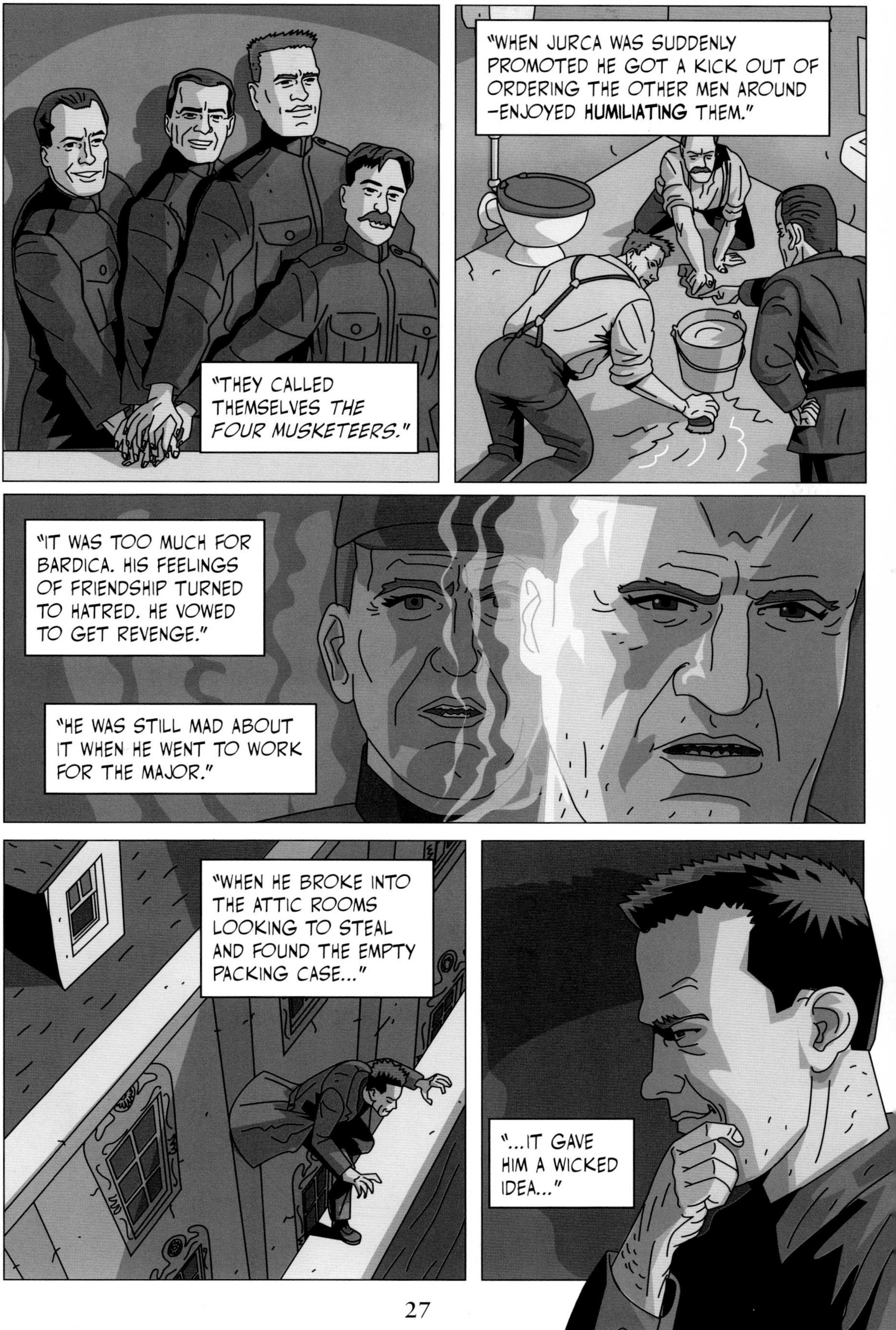
"THEY CALLED THEMSELVES THE FOUR MUSKETEERS."
"WHEN JURCA WAS SUDDENLY PROMOTED HE GOT A KICK OUT OF ORDERING THE OTHER MEN AROUND —ENJOYED HUMILIATING THEM."
"IT WAS TOO MUCH FOR BARDICA. HIS FEELINGS OF FRIENDSHIP TURNED TO HATRED. HE VOWED TO GET REVENGE."
"HE WAS STILL MAD ABOUT IT WHEN HE WENT TO WORK FOR THE MAJOR."
"WHEN HE BROKE INTO THE ATTIC ROOMS LOOKING TO STEAL AND FOUND THE EMPTY PACKING CASE..."
"...IT GAVE HIM A WICKED IDEA..."

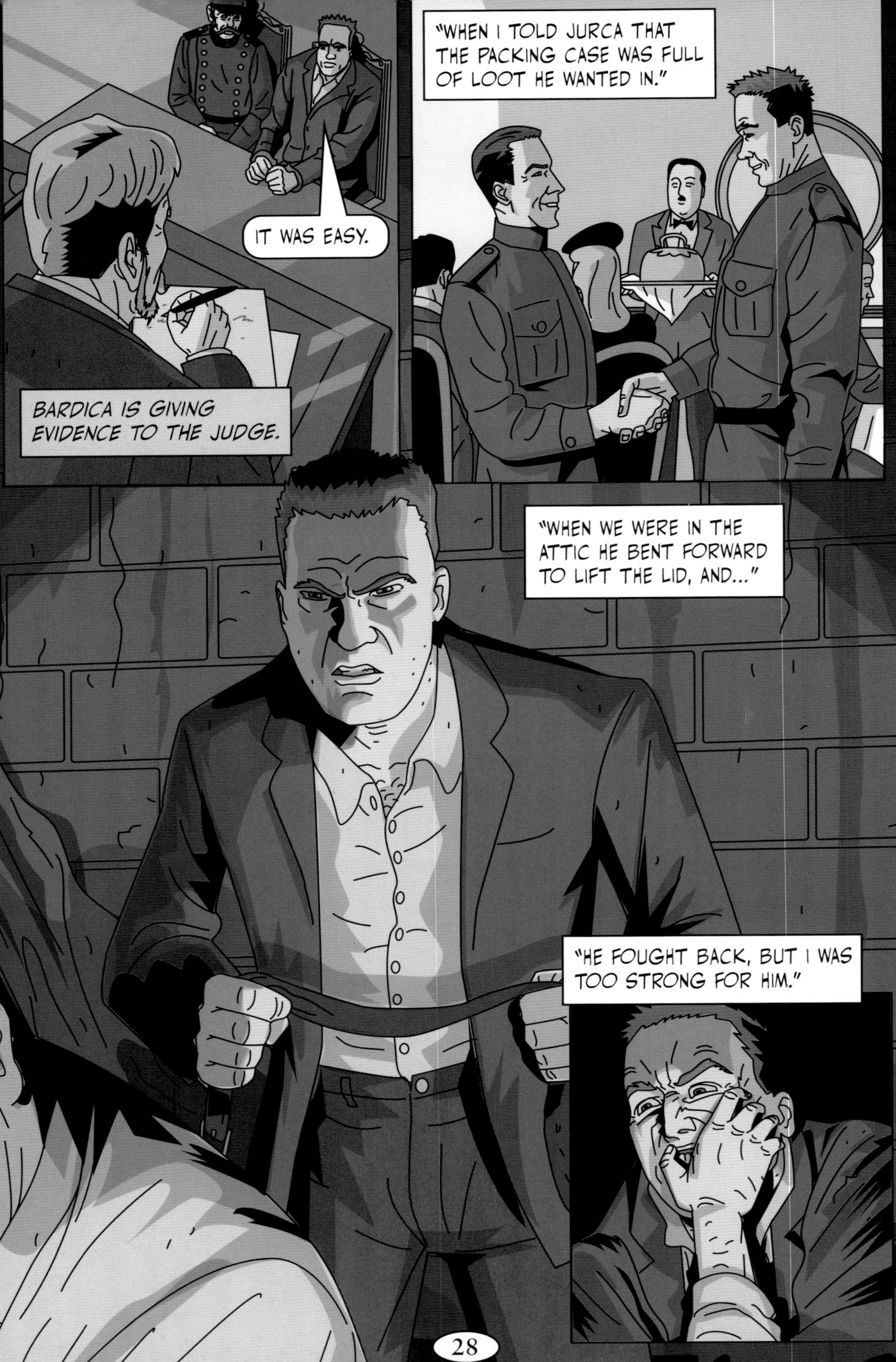

BARDICA IS GIVING EVIDENCE TO THE JUDGE.
IT WAS EASY.
"WHEN I TOLD JURCA THAT THE PACKING CASE WAS FULL OF LOOT HE WANTED IN."
"WHEN WE WERE IN THE ATTIC HE BENT FORWARD TO LIFT THE LID, AND..."
"HE FOUGHT BACK, BUT I WAS TOO STRONG FOR HIM."

WHY DID YOU WAIT TWO WEEKS TO REMOVE THE BODY?

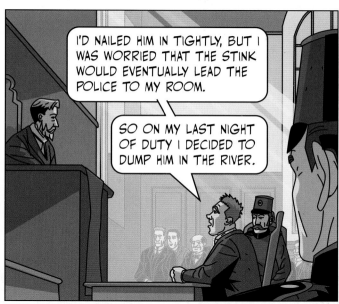

I'D NAILED HIM IN TIGHTLY, BUT I WAS WORRIED THAT THE STINK WOULD EVENTUALLY LEAD THE POLICE TO MY ROOM.

SO ON MY LAST NIGHT OF DUTY I DECIDED TO DUMP HIM IN THE RIVER.

"I HAD TO DRAG HIM DOWN THE STAIRS, WHICH WOKE A WOMAN UP. LUCKILY FOR HER, SHE DIDN'T COME OUT."

WHO'S THERE?

"WHEN I FOUND THAT THE GATES WERE LOCKED I GAVE UP AND LEFT HIM FOR THE COPS TO FIND."

I THOUGHT I'D BE SAFE. I DIDN'T THINK THERE WAS ANYTHING ON HIM THAT COULD LINK HIM TO ME.

THE END

THE COLD CASE

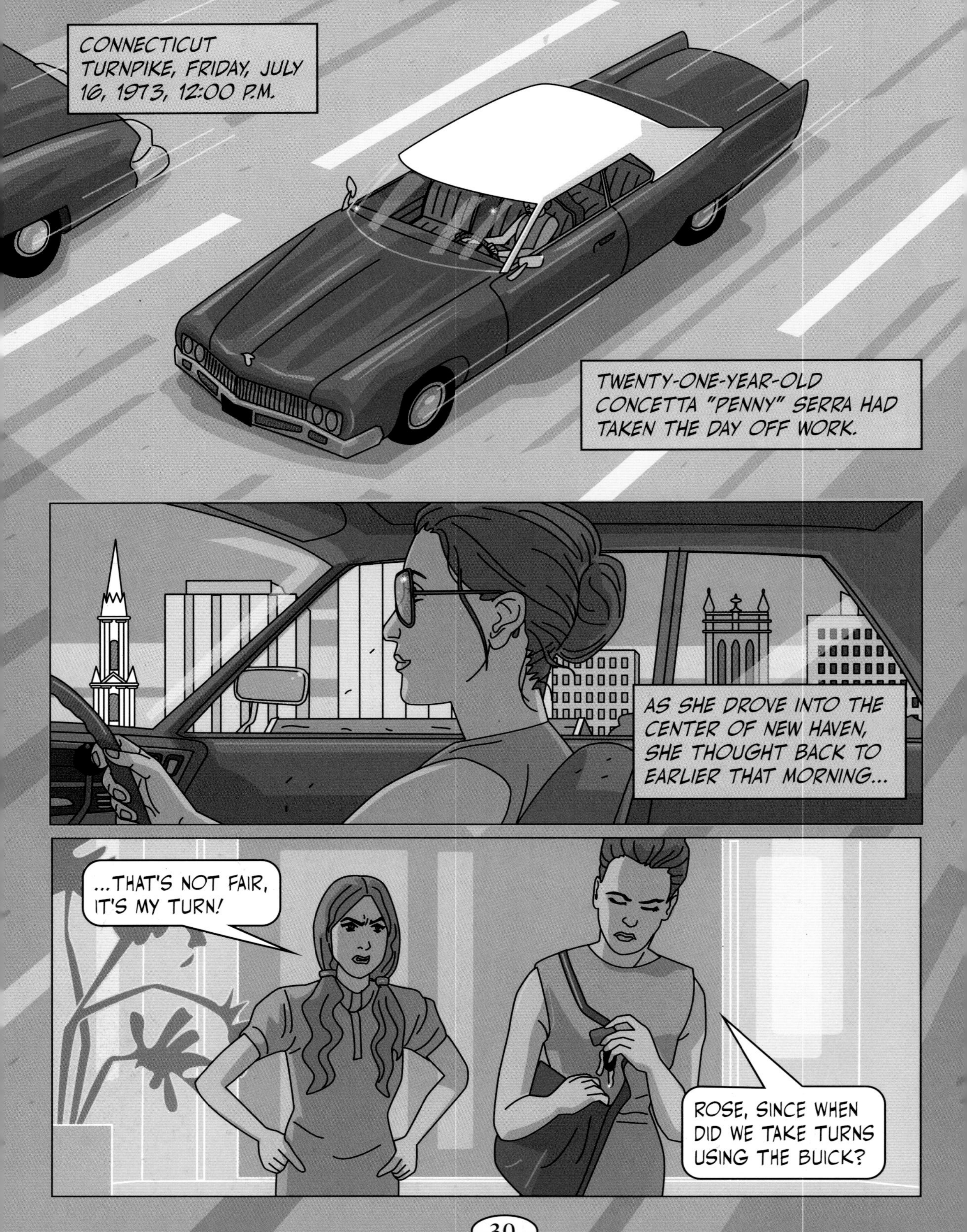
CONNECTICUT TURNPIKE, FRIDAY, JULY 16, 1973, 12:00 P.M.
TWENTY-ONE-YEAR-OLD CONCETTA "PENNY" SERRA HAD TAKEN THE DAY OFF WORK.
AS SHE DROVE INTO THE CENTER OF NEW HAVEN, SHE THOUGHT BACK TO EARLIER THAT MORNING...
...THAT'S NOT FAIR, IT'S MY TURN!
ROSE, SINCE WHEN DID WE TAKE TURNS USING THE BUICK?

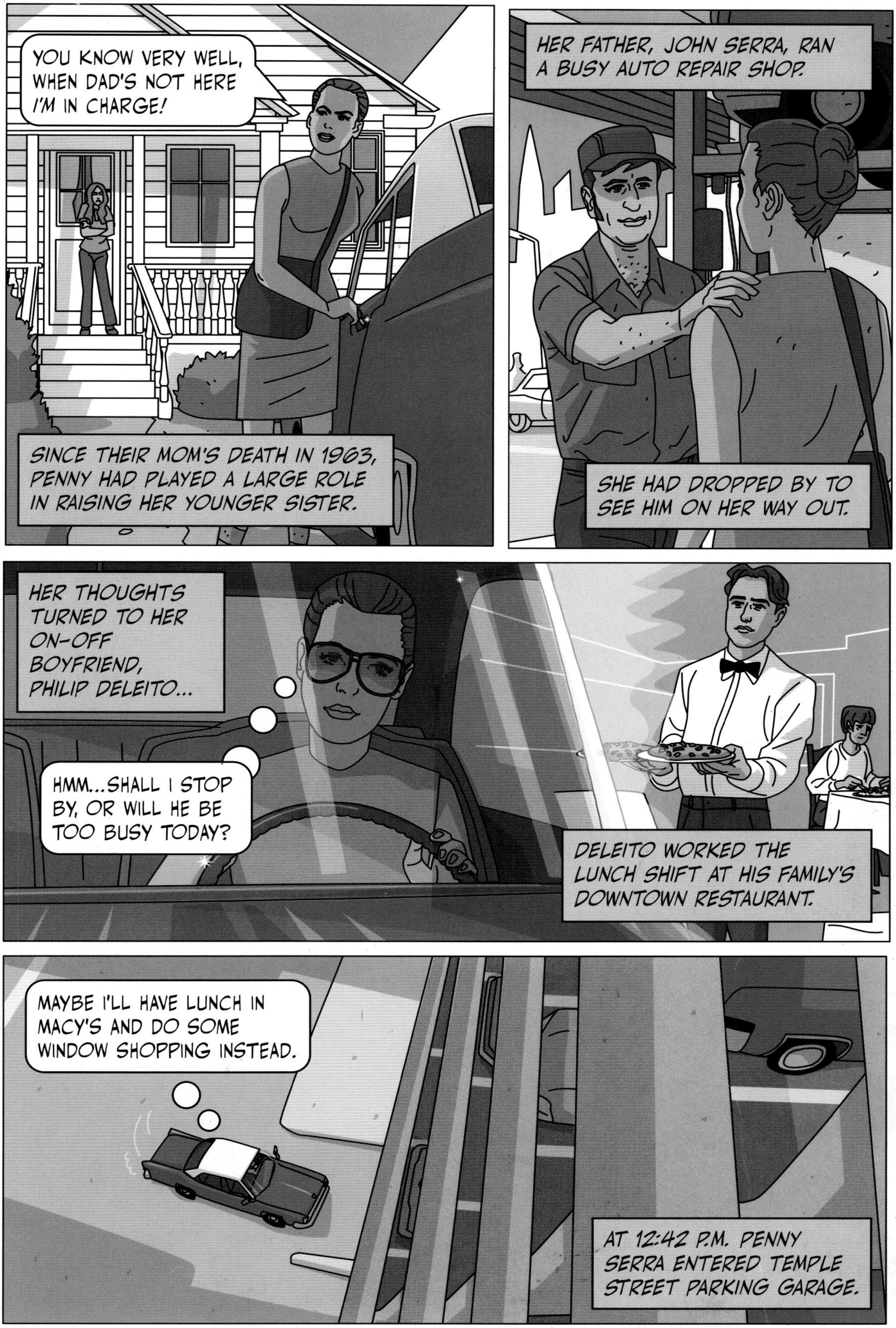
YOU KNOW VERY WELL, WHEN DAD'S NOT HERE I'M IN CHARGE!
SINCE THEIR MOM'S DEATH IN 1963, PENNY HAD PLAYED A LARGE ROLE IN RAISING HER YOUNGER SISTER.
HER FATHER, JOHN SERRA, RAN A BUSY AUTO REPAIR SHOP.
SHE HAD DROPPED BY TO SEE HIM ON HER WAY OUT.
HER THOUGHTS TURNED TO HER ON-OFF BOYFRIEND, PHILIP DELEITO...
HMM...SHALL I STOP BY, OR WILL HE BE TOO BUSY TODAY?
DELEITO WORKED THE LUNCH SHIFT AT HIS FAMILY'S DOWNTOWN RESTAURANT.
MAYBE I'LL HAVE LUNCH IN MACY'S AND DO SOME WINDOW SHOPPING INSTEAD.
AT 12:42 P.M. PENNY SERRA ENTERED TEMPLE STREET PARKING GARAGE.

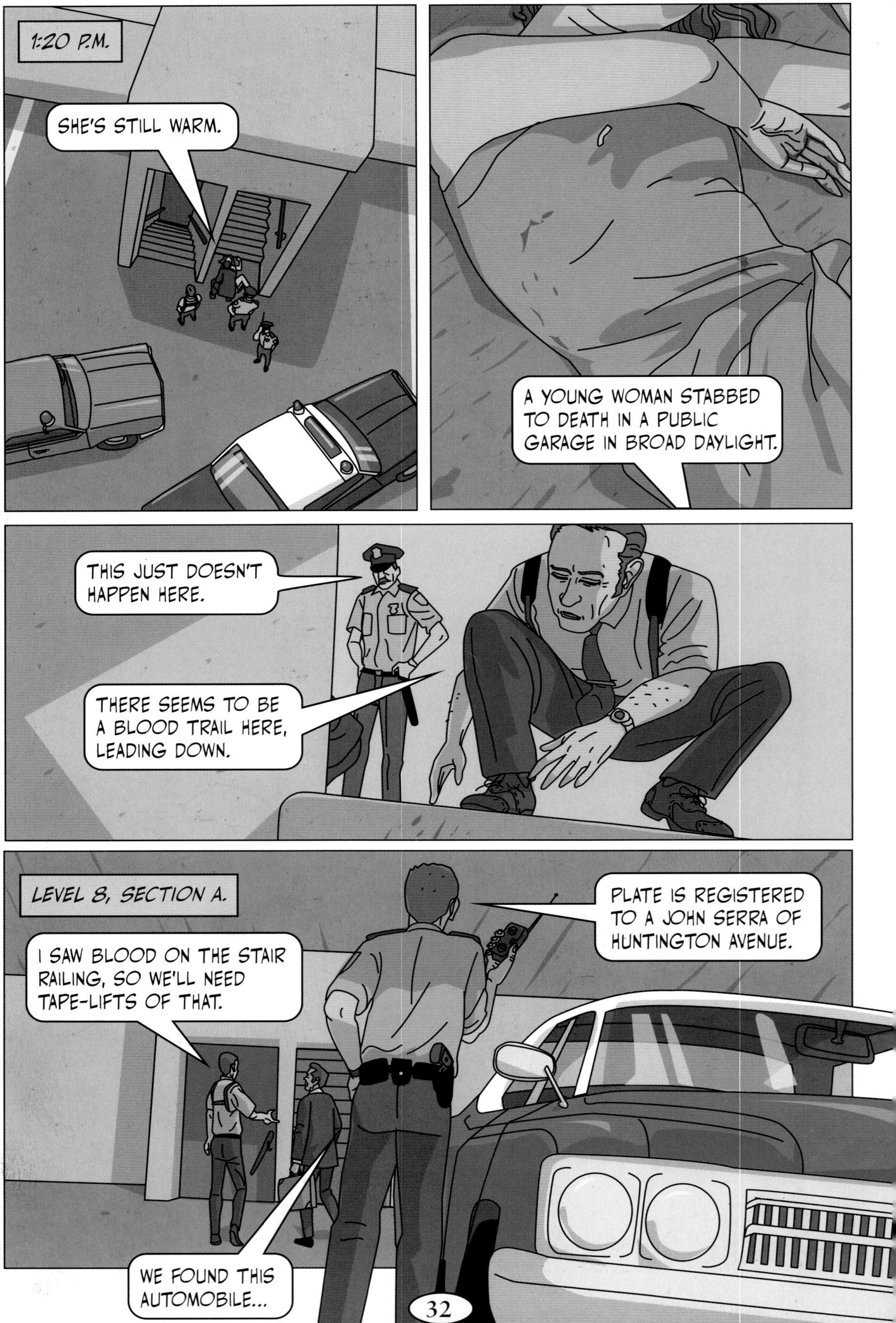
1:20 P.M.
SHE'S STILL WARM.
A YOUNG WOMAN STABBED TO DEATH IN A PUBLIC GARAGE IN BROAD DAYLIGHT.
THIS JUST DOESN'T HAPPEN HERE.
THERE SEEMS TO BE A BLOOD TRAIL HERE, LEADING DOWN.
LEVEL 8, SECTION A.
I SAW BLOOD ON THE STAIR RAILING, SO WE'LL NEED TAPE-LIFTS OF THAT.
PLATE IS REGISTERED TO A JOHN SERRA OF HUNTINGTON AVENUE.
WE FOUND THIS AUTOMOBILE...

FOUND A WALLET—FOURTEEN DOLLARS, SEVENTY-FIVE CENTS. AND DRIVER'S LICENSE FOR CONCETTA SERRA.

CONNECTICUT STATE
DRIVER LICENSE

THERE'S BLOOD ALL OVER THE STEERING COLUMN, BUT NO SIGN OF THE KEYS.

WE'LL NEED THE EVIDENCE GUYS TO DO A REAL THOROUGH JOB ON THIS ONE...

BEHIND THE DRIVER'S SEAT EVIDENCE TECHNICIANS FIND A RAG...

...LIKE THE KIND USED IN AUTO SHOPS.

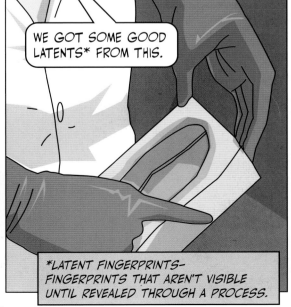

WE GOT SOME GOOD LATENTS* FROM THIS.

*LATENT FINGERPRINTS— FINGERPRINTS THAT AREN'T VISIBLE UNTIL REVEALED THROUGH A PROCESS.

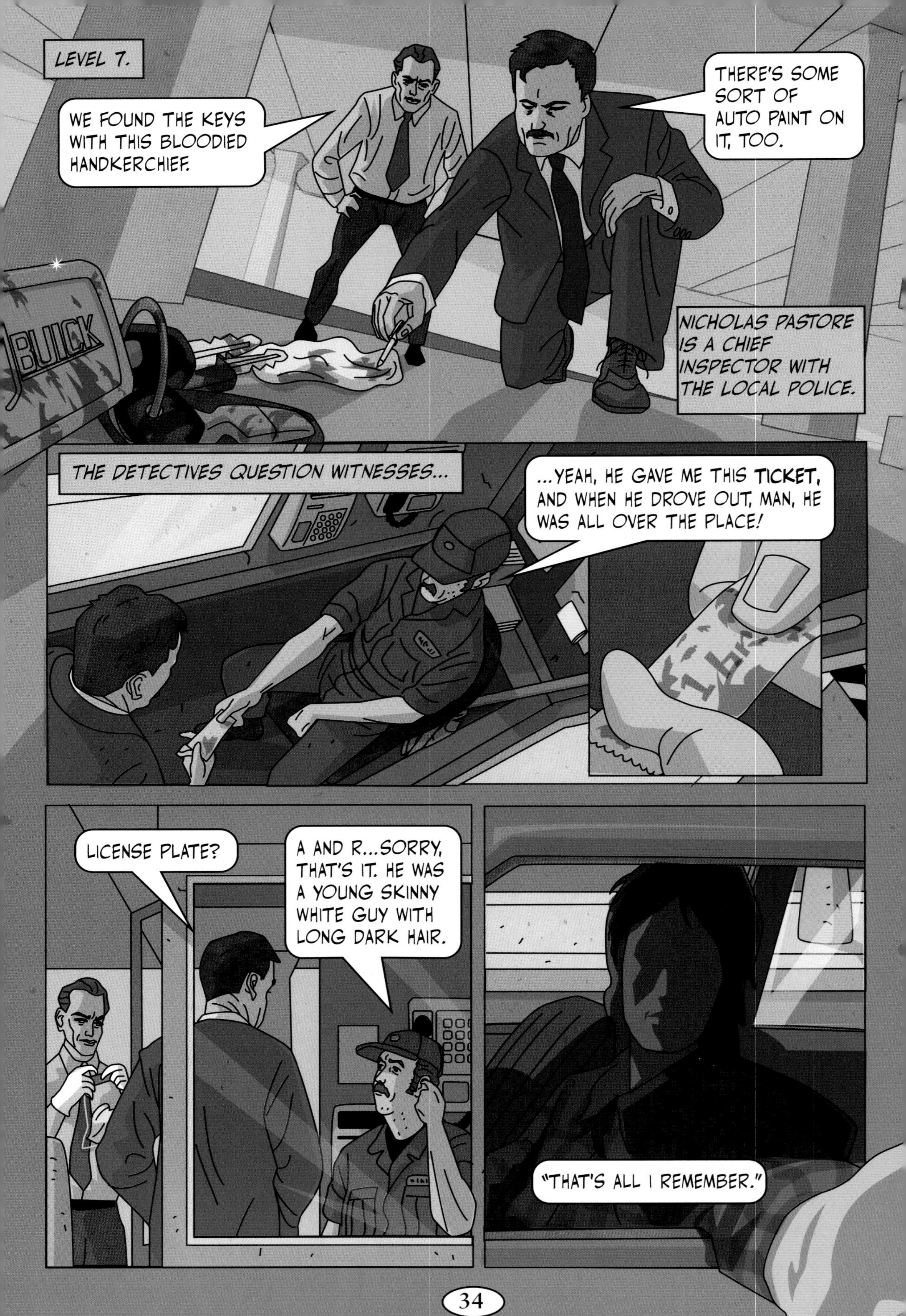
LEVEL 7.
WE FOUND THE KEYS WITH THIS BLOODIED HANDKERCHIEF.
THERE'S SOME SORT OF AUTO PAINT ON IT, TOO.
BUICK
NICHOLAS PASTORE IS A CHIEF INSPECTOR WITH THE LOCAL POLICE.
THE DETECTIVES QUESTION WITNESSES...
...YEAH, HE GAVE ME THIS **TICKET**, AND WHEN HE DROVE OUT, MAN, HE WAS ALL OVER THE PLACE!
LICENSE PLATE?
A AND R...SORRY, THAT'S IT. HE WAS A YOUNG SKINNY WHITE GUY WITH LONG DARK HAIR.
"THAT'S ALL I REMEMBER."

AFTER HE TAKES PART IN A POLICE LINEUP, SERRA'S BOYFRIEND, DELEITO, IS EXCLUDED FROM THE INVESTIGATION.

THAT RULES OUT A CRIME OF PASSION.

MOST LIKELY A STRANGER CRIME, THEN.

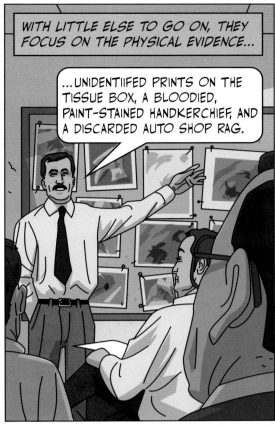

WITH LITTLE ELSE TO GO ON, THEY FOCUS ON THE PHYSICAL EVIDENCE...

...UNIDENTIIFED PRINTS ON THE TISSUE BOX, A BLOODIED, PAINT-STAINED HANDKERCHIEF, AND A DISCARDED AUTO SHOP RAG.

HOWEVER, THERE ARE MORE THAN 2,500 AUTO REPAIR SHOPS IN THE NEW HAVEN AREA ALONE.

ANOTHER STRIKEOUT —THIS IS GOING TO TAKE MONTHS, IF NOT YEARS!

THE FINGERPRINTS REMAIN UNMATCHED, AND DESPITE ALL THE BLOOD EVIDENCE...

...ALL WE KNOW IS THAT THE VICTIM HAD TYPE A BLOOD AND THE ASSAILANT'S, FOUND IN THE GARAGE AND THE CAR, IS TYPE O.

DESPITE THEIR BEST EFFORTS, THE SERRA CASE IS BEGINNING TO APPEAR *UNSOLVABLE*.

HUNTINGTON AVENUE, NEW HAVEN, JULY, 1974.

NEW HAVEN REGISTER, CLASSIFIED SECTION, HOW MAY I HELP?

I'D LIKE TO PLACE AN ADVERTISEMENT PLEASE. TEXT AS FOLLOWS...

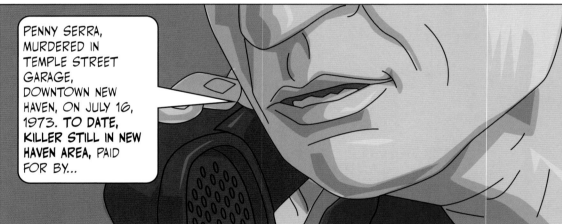

PENNY SERRA, MURDERED IN TEMPLE STREET GARAGE, DOWNTOWN NEW HAVEN, ON JULY 16, 1973. **TO DATE, KILLER STILL IN NEW HAVEN AREA,** PAID FOR BY...

...JOHN SERRA.

FOR THE NEXT TWENTY-FIVE YEARS, JOHN SERRA CONTINUES TO PLACE REGULAR ADS IN THE NEW HAVEN REGISTER, KEEPING THE CASE IN THE PUBLIC EYE.

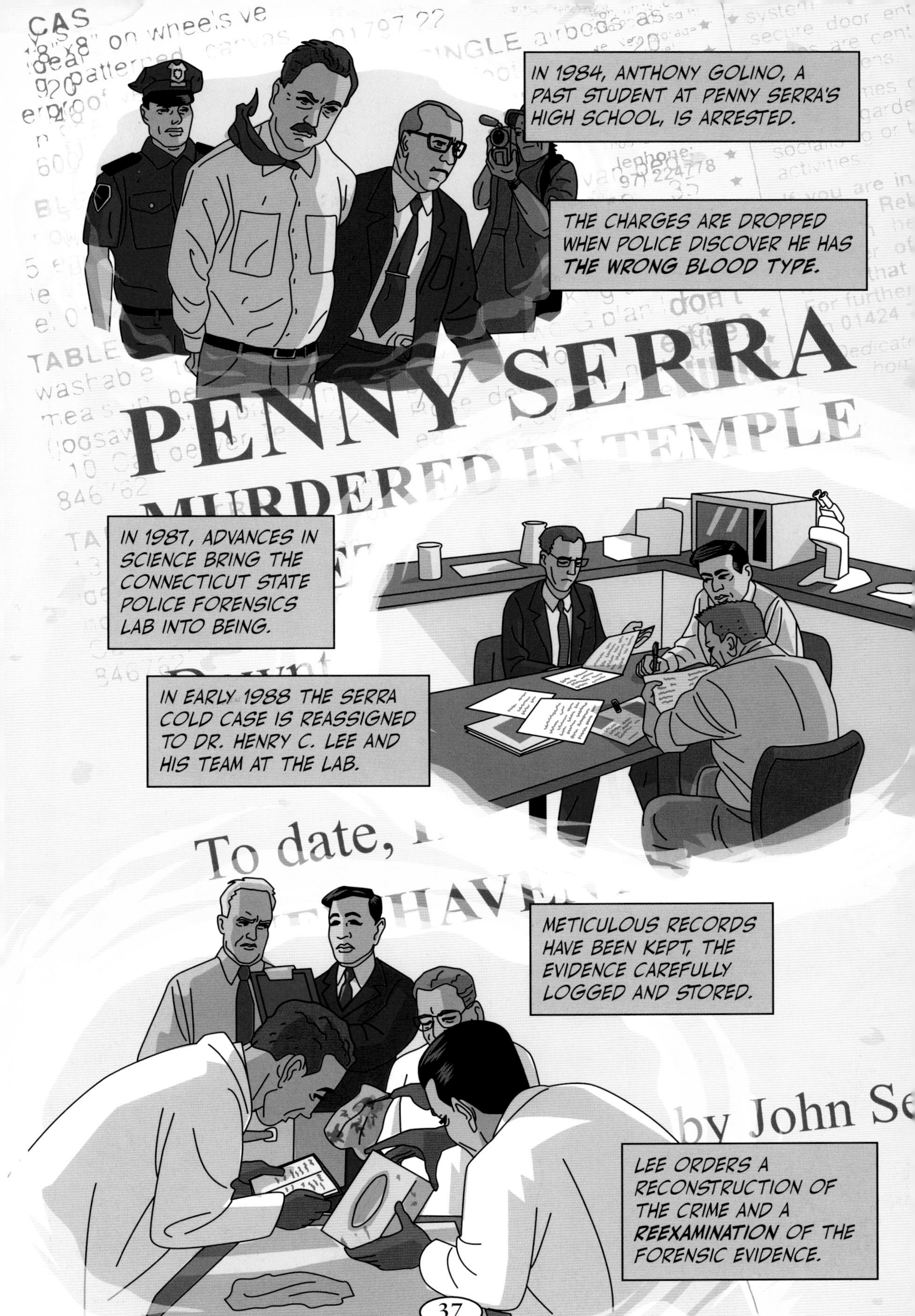
IN 1984, ANTHONY GOLINO, A PAST STUDENT AT PENNY SERRA'S HIGH SCHOOL, IS ARRESTED.
THE CHARGES ARE DROPPED WHEN POLICE DISCOVER HE HAS THE WRONG BLOOD TYPE.
PENNY SERRA
MURDERED IN TEMPLE
IN 1987, ADVANCES IN SCIENCE BRING THE CONNECTICUT STATE POLICE FORENSICS LAB INTO BEING.
IN EARLY 1988 THE SERRA COLD CASE IS REASSIGNED TO DR. HENRY C. LEE AND HIS TEAM AT THE LAB.
To date,
METICULOUS RECORDS HAVE BEEN KEPT, THE EVIDENCE CAREFULLY LOGGED AND STORED.
by John Se
LEE ORDERS A RECONSTRUCTION OF THE CRIME AND A REEXAMINATION OF THE FORENSIC EVIDENCE.

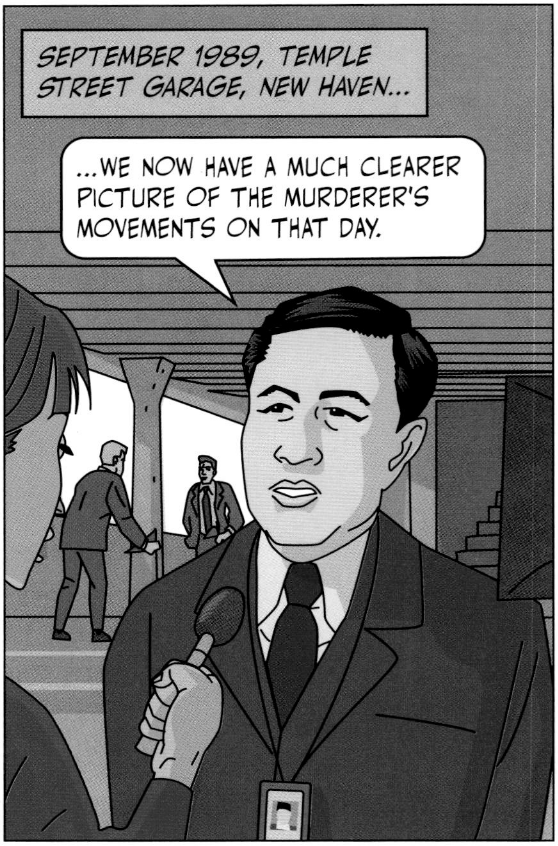
SEPTEMBER 1989, TEMPLE STREET GARAGE, NEW HAVEN...
...WE NOW HAVE A MUCH CLEARER PICTURE OF THE MURDERER'S MOVEMENTS ON THAT DAY.

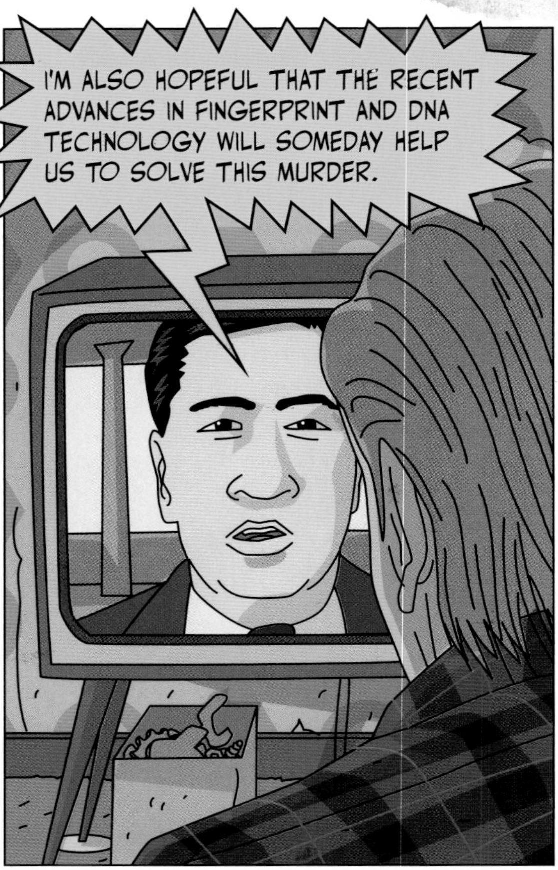
I'M ALSO HOPEFUL THAT THE RECENT ADVANCES IN FINGERPRINT AND DNA TECHNOLOGY WILL SOMEDAY HELP US TO SOLVE THIS MURDER.

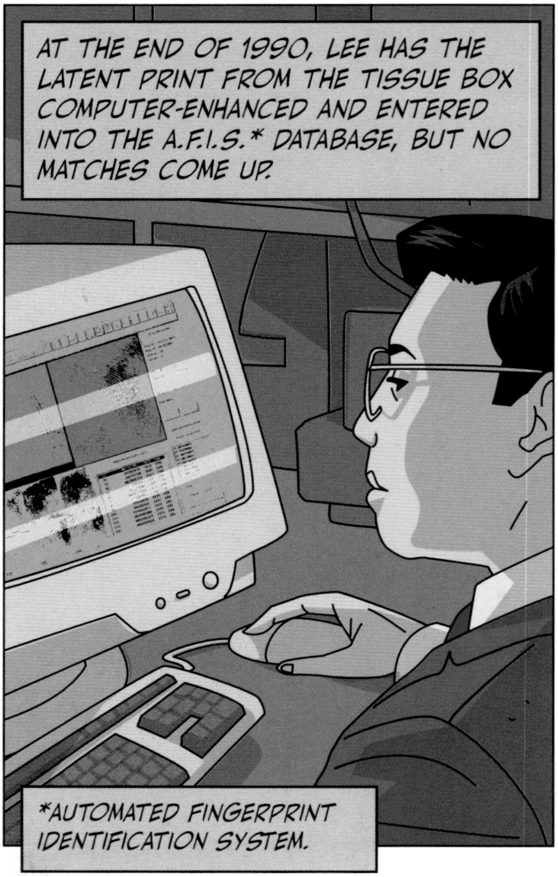
AT THE END OF 1990, LEE HAS THE LATENT PRINT FROM THE TISSUE BOX COMPUTER-ENHANCED AND ENTERED INTO THE A.F.I.S.* DATABASE, BUT NO MATCHES COME UP.
*AUTOMATED FINGERPRINT IDENTIFICATION SYSTEM.

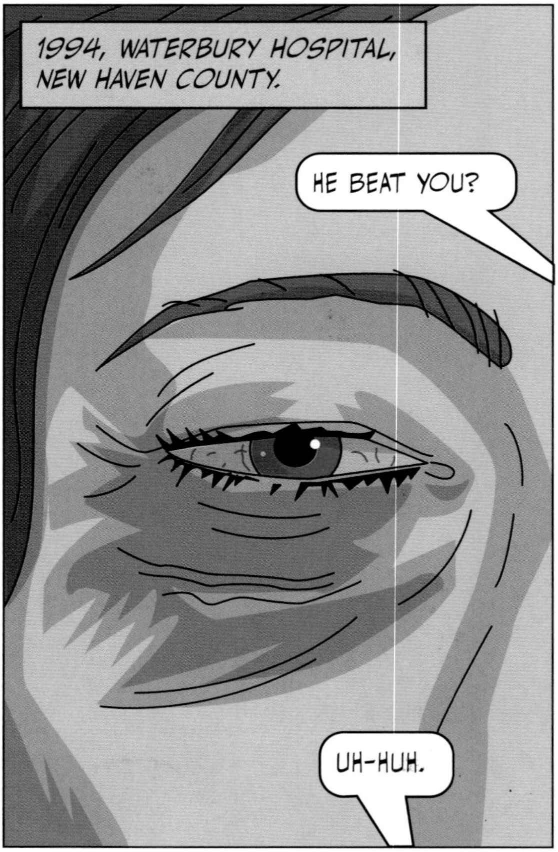
1994, WATERBURY HOSPITAL, NEW HAVEN COUNTY.
HE BEAT YOU?
UH-HUH.

DO YOU WANT US TO CALL THE POLICE?

YES.

THE WOMAN'S FIANCÉ, EDWARD GRANT, IS ARRESTED AND FINGERPRINTED, ALTHOUGH THE CHARGES ARE LATER DROPPED.

HOLD STILL, PLEASE.

AT A CONNECTICUT/RHODE ISLAND FINGERPRINT DATABASE IN 1997...

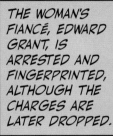

subject: Edward R. Grant
left thumbprint
matched with a partial from
Concetta Serra murder case

MATCH!

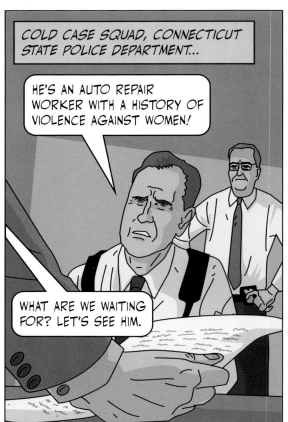

COLD CASE SQUAD, CONNECTICUT STATE POLICE DEPARTMENT...

HE'S AN AUTO REPAIR WORKER WITH A HISTORY OF VIOLENCE AGAINST WOMEN!

WHAT ARE WE WAITING FOR? LET'S SEE HIM.

I HAVE NO IDEA HOW MY FINGERPRINT COULD HAVE GOTTEN IN THERE.

THERE'S A REALLY EASY WAY YOU COULD RULE YOURSELF OUT OF THIS ENTIRE INVESTIGATION.

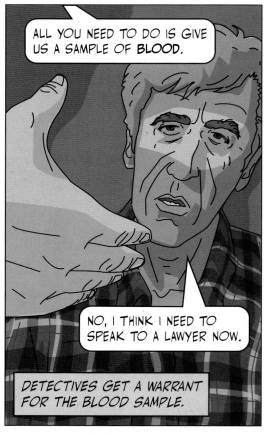

ALL YOU NEED TO DO IS GIVE US A SAMPLE OF BLOOD.

NO, I THINK I NEED TO SPEAK TO A LAWYER NOW.

DETECTIVES GET A WARRANT FOR THE BLOOD SAMPLE.

WHEN GRANT'S DNA IS ANALYZED AND COMPARED AGAINST DNA FROM THE TYPE OF BLOOD RETRIEVED AT THE SCENE...

IT'S A MATCH!

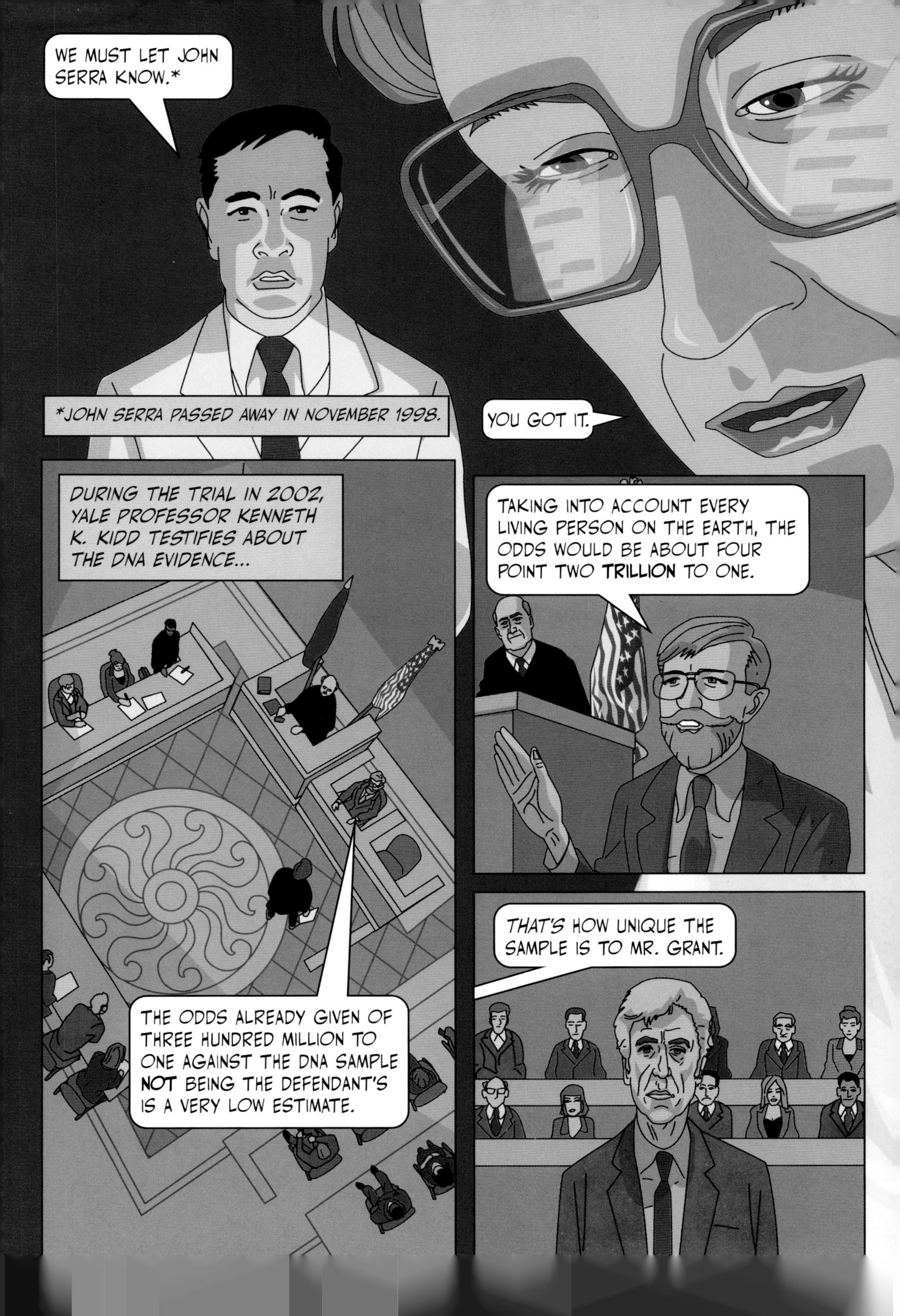
WE MUST LET JOHN SERRA KNOW.*
*JOHN SERRA PASSED AWAY IN NOVEMBER 1998.
YOU GOT IT.
DURING THE TRIAL IN 2002, YALE PROFESSOR KENNETH K. KIDD TESTIFIES ABOUT THE DNA EVIDENCE...
THE ODDS ALREADY GIVEN OF THREE HUNDRED MILLION TO ONE AGAINST THE DNA SAMPLE NOT BEING THE DEFENDANT'S IS A VERY LOW ESTIMATE.
TAKING INTO ACCOUNT EVERY LIVING PERSON ON THE EARTH, THE ODDS WOULD BE ABOUT FOUR POINT TWO TRILLION TO ONE.
THAT'S HOW UNIQUE THE SAMPLE IS TO MR. GRANT.

LATER, DR. LEE TALKS ABOUT THE CRIME SCENE...

THE INCIDENT BEGAN WHEN EDWARD GRANT THREATENED OR ATTACKED MISS SERRA AS SHE PARKED HER CAR ON THE NINTH FLOOR.

↑TO LEVEL 10

"DURING THE STRUGGLE, MR. GRANT WAS WOUNDED IN HIS LEFT HAND. MISS SERRA THEN RAN TO THE TENTH FLOOR, WITH MR. GRANT IN PURSUIT."

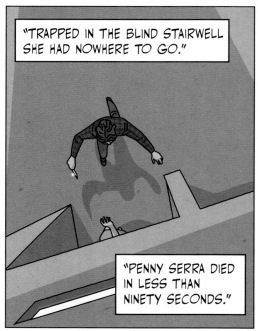

"TRAPPED IN THE BLIND STAIRWELL SHE HAD NOWHERE TO GO."

"PENNY SERRA DIED IN LESS THAN NINETY SECONDS."

"STILL BLEEDING, GRANT DROVE THE BUICK TO THE EIGHTH LEVEL, REACHING BEHIND THE SEAT FOR TISSUES TO STANCH HIS WOUND."

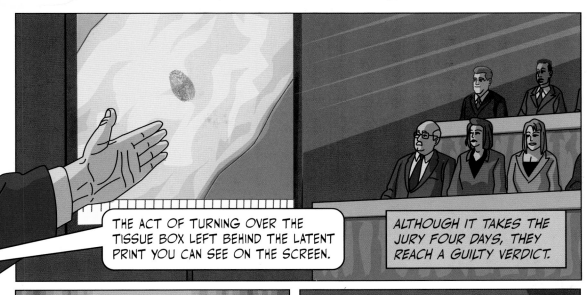

THE ACT OF TURNING OVER THE TISSUE BOX LEFT BEHIND THE LATENT PRINT YOU CAN SEE ON THE SCREEN.

ALTHOUGH IT TAKES THE JURY FOUR DAYS, THEY REACH A GUILTY VERDICT.

AT THE SENTENCING THE DEFENDANT SPEAKS...

I DIDN'T *MURDER* PENNY SERRA, BUT I DO FEEL SORRY FOR ALL THE SUFFERING THE FAMILY HAS ENDURED.

JUDGE BLUE IS PRESIDING...

ALL THE PERFUMES OF ARABIA WILL NOT SWEETEN YOUR BLOODSTAINED HANDS! YOU WILL SERVE TWENTY TO LIFE.

ROSEMARY SERRA HAS THE FINAL SAY...

IF YOU HAD COME FORWARD TWENTY-NINE YEARS AGO, MAYBE I WOULD NOT HAVE HAD TO LOOK INTO MY FATHER'S HAUNTED EYES.

YOU TURNED TIME INTO OUR *ENEMY.*

THE END

OTHER FAMOUS CASES

Here are some other celebrated cases that relied on forensic trace evidence to help solve a crime.

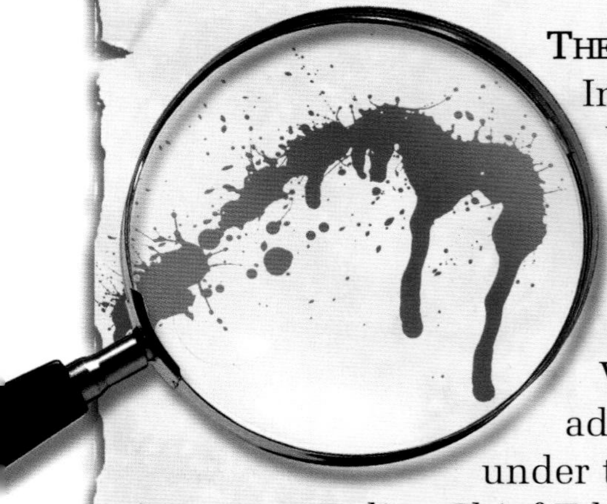

The Francisca Rojas Case

In 1891 in Argentina, an official, Juan Vucetich, set up a basic fingerprint classification system. The following year, two children were found at home battered to death. The mother, Francisca Rojas, accused a neighbor, Pedro Ramon Velasquez, of being the killer. Velasquez admitted he once threatened her but even under torture said he was innocent. Police Chief Eduardo Alvarez suspected Francisca. Examining the murder scene closely, he found a bloody thumbprint.

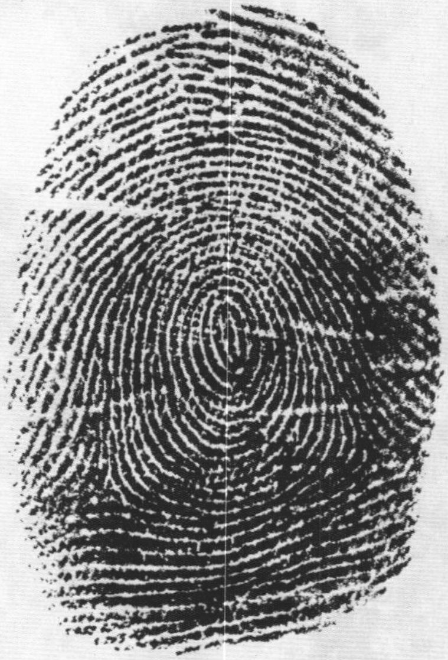

Comparision with Francisca's thumbprint proved it was hers, and she'd already denied touching the bodies. Confronted with the evidence, she confessed she had killed her children to be free to marry a much younger man. Rojas was the first person found guilty by fingerprint evidence.

The Mail Train Murders

Following a botched train robbery in 1923 in Oregon, a local mechanic was arrested for the murder of three railroad employees. The evidence, a pair of grease-stained overalls found at the scene, was given to forensics Professor Oscar Heinrich. He told the police that they had the wrong man. Trace evidence on the overalls had shown that the assailant was a brown-haired, left-handed lumberjack, twenty-one to twenty-five years old, five feet ten inches tall, and of meticulous habits.

The grease was fir pitch, and a brown hair was caught in a buttonhole. Precise nail clippings were in the right-hand pocket. The information helped catch the perpetrator a month later.

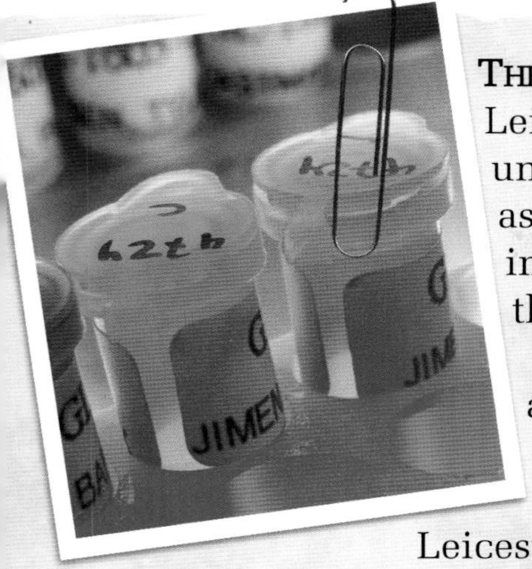
JIMEN

The Pitchfork Murder Case

Leicester, United Kingdom, 1987. An unsolved murder case involving separate assaults of two girls, one in 1983 and one in 1986, less than a mile apart was taxing the police.

A seventeen-year-old youth had been arrested on flimsy evidence. Needing proof detectives had sent a sample of his saliva to the lab of Dr. Alec Jeffreys at Leicester University. Jeffreys had developed a new identification test using DNA. However, when the youth's DNA profile was compared with the profile based on evidence collected from the bodies, it did not match.

In desperation the police randomly tested 5,000 males in the local area, again with no result. The case was looking unsolvable when someone overheard a man bragging about fooling the police by supplying a false blood sample for his friend. The friend, Colin Pitchfork, was quickly arrested.

By the time his positive lab match came back he had confessed to the crimes. Pitchfork was the first person found guilty of homicide through DNA fingerprinting.

Feline Witness

The first time animal DNA was used to solve a crime was in Canada in 1994. The body of a missing thirty-two-year-old, Shirley Duguay, was found on Prince Edward Island. Her estranged common-law husband, Doug Beamish, was the prime suspect. A bloodstained jacket suspected of being his had been found near the body, but no family members would testify that he owned it.

White hairs on the jacket were carefully examined and turned out to belong to a cat. Mounties recalled that a white cat named Snowball lived at Beamish's parents' house. They had Snowball's blood tested and found his DNA matched the hair's. Beamish was convicted of second-degree murder.

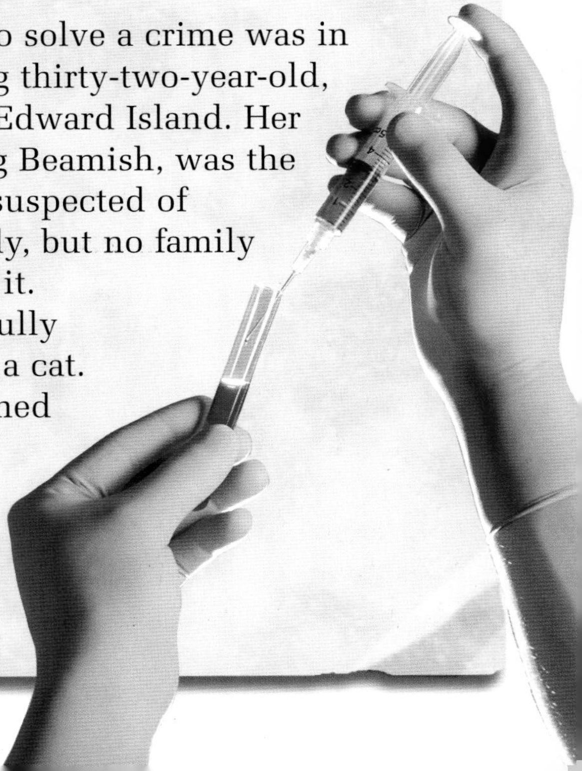

GLOSSARY

analysis Detailed examination of the parts that make up a piece of evidence.

assailant A person who attacks another.

circumstantial Evidence that points indirectly to a person's guilt, but does not prove it.

classify To arrange fingerprints into groups based on shared patterns.

conscript One who is drafted, or forced, to join a group.

comparison The comparing of one fingerprint with another.

confession A written or oral statement, acknowledging guilt.

dactyloscopy The science of comparing fingerprints to make an identification.

enhancement Improvement of the quality of a partial fingerprint.

meticulous To be extremely careful and precise.

microscopy The use of a microscope for analysis.

New Scotland Yard Headquarters of Greater London Metropolitan Police Force.

partial print An incomplete or smudged fingerprint.

post-mortem A medical examination of a dead body.

precise Highly accurate.

principle A basic truth.

remand To return to custody or detention.

serology Scientific study of blood.

spectroscope A machine for producing and analyzing the light given off by different materials.

stanch Stop the flow of.

tape-lift A technique used to preserve and transport a sample for later microscopy.

testify To make a declaration of truth under oath.

toxins Natural and human-made poisons that cause disease.

warrant A judicial writ, authorizing an officer to make a search, a seizure, or an arrest.

FOR MORE INFORMATION

ORGANIZATIONS

International Crime Scene Investigators Association
PMB 385
15774 S. LaGrange Road
Orland Park, IL 60462
(708) 460-8082
Web site: http://www.icsia.org

The FBI Academy
Forensic Science Research & Training Center
Hoover Road
Quantico, VA 22135
(703) 632 1000
Web site: http://www.fbi.gov

FOR FURTHER READING

Campbell, Andrea. *Forensic Science: Evidence, Clues, and Investigation.* New York, NY: Chelsea House Publishers, 1999.

Friedlander, Mark P. Jr., and Terry Phillips. *When Objects Talk: Solving a Crime with Science.* Breckenridge, CO: Twenty-First Century Books, 2001.

Rollins, Barbara B., and Michael Dahl. *Blood Evidence.* Mankato, MN: Capstone Press, 2004.

Rollins, Barbara B., and Michael Dahl. *Fingerprint Evidence.* Mankato, MN: Capstone Press, 2004.

Yeatts, Tabitha. *Forensics: Solving the Crime.* Minneapolis, MN: Oliver Press, 2001.

INDEX

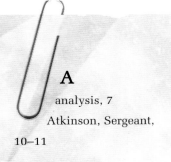

Web Sites

Due to the changing nature of Internet links, Rosen Publishing has developed an online list of Web sites related to the subject of this book. This site is updated regularly. Please use this link to access the list:

http://www.rosenlinks.com/gfs/dfte